Comments on other *Amazing* ...eaders & reviewers

"*You might call them the non-fiction response to Harlequin romances: easy to consume and potentially addictive.*"
Robert Martin, *The Chronicle Herald*

"*Tightly written volumes filled with lots of wit and humour about famous and infamous Canadians.*"
Eric Shackleton, *The Globe and Mail*

"*This is popular history as it should be... For this price, buy two and give one to a friend.*"
Terry Cook, a reader from Ottawa, on **Rebel Women**

"*Stories are rich in description, and bristle with a clever, stylish realness.*"
Mark Weber, *Central Alberta Advisor,* on **Ghost Town Stories II**

"*The resulting book is one readers will want to share with all the women in their lives.*"
Lynn Martel, *Rocky Mountain Outlook,* on **Women Explorers**

"[The books are] *long on plot and character and short on the sort of technical analysis that can be dreary for all but the most committed academic.*"
Robert Martin, *The Chronicle Herald*

"*A compelling read. Bertin...has selected only the most intriguing tales, which she narrates with a wealth of detail.*"
Joyce Glasner, *New Brunswick Reader,* on **Strange Events**

"*The heightened sense of drama and intrigue, combined with a good dose of human interest is what sets* Amazing Stories *apart.*"
Pamela Klaffke, *Calgary Herald*

GREAT RAILWAYS OF THE CANADIAN WEST

AMAZING STORIES®

GREAT RAILWAYS OF THE CANADIAN WEST

Building the Dream That Shaped Our Nation

HISTORY

by Graeme Pole

PUBLISHED BY ALTITUDE PUBLISHING CANADA LTD.
1500 Railway Avenue, Canmore, Alberta T1W 1P6
www.altitudepublishing.com
1-800-957-6888

Extreme care has been taken to ensure that all information presented in
this book is accurate and up to date. Neither the author nor the
publisher can be held responsible for any errors.

Publisher	Stephen Hutchings
Associate Publisher	Kara Turner
Editor	Gayl Veinotte
Cover and layout	Bryan Pezzi
Maps	Scott Manktelow

We acknowledge the financial support of the Government
of Canada through the Book Publishing Industry Development
Program (BPIDP) for our publishing activities.

Altitude GreenTree Program
Altitude Publishing will plant twice as many trees as were used
in the manufacturing of this product.

Library and Archives Canada Cataloguing in Publication

Pole, Graeme, 1956-
   Great Railways of the Canadian West / Graeme Pole.

(Amazing stories)
Includes bibliographical references.
ISBN 1-55439-062-1

   1. Railroads--Canada, Western--History. I. Title. II. Series:
Amazing stories (Canmore, Alta.)

HE2808.P64 2005   385'.09712   C2005-905742-4

Printed and bound in Canada by Friesens
2 4 6 8 9 7 5 3 1

"There is no branch of the organization of a country —
political, municipal, social, or constructive — to the
success of which a good map is not essential."
Millington Henry Synge, 1852

"The work of an engineer on construction
is but little understood by the general public.
Some doubtless regard him as simply a fellow who looks
through a telescope and sees things upside down."
P. Turner Bone, 1947

Contents

Prologue

In the autumn of 1883, surveyor Charles Shaw received a desperate assignment. Track-laying for the Canadian Pacific Railway (CPR) was proceeding apace through the Bow Valley, aiming for the eastern approach to Kicking Horse Pass in the Rocky Mountains. To the west of the pass, the railway's proposed route plunged into the Kicking Horse Valley. Avalanche slopes scoured the canyon-rent course for most of the 50 miles to the Columbia River. Major A.B. Rogers had surveyed the route in 1882 and had staked his reputation on it, but no one else involved with the CPR believed it was viable.

Word came from the company's head office in Montreal: If there was a better way, find it. Shaw's boss dispatched him to make a reconnaissance survey of Howse Pass, the next major break through the mountains north of Kicking Horse Pass. In the Howse Valley, Shaw investigated a series of tributaries, but each ended at "a glacier in high, rugged peaks." He reported that "we were reduced to something less than half rations," so he travelled alone, not wanting to subject his men to the hardship of travel on empty stomachs.

When Shaw finally found Howse Pass, he and his brother Norman took six biscuits and two blankets and set off to make a tentative crossing. Frigid rain soon drenched them, forcing a bivouac.

Next day, while Norman dried the blankets, Shaw crossed the pass, but the tangle of forest on the west side of the Continental Divide stopped him. The biscuits gone, he and Norman hiked through the night back to camp, where they found renewed orders to run a trial line across any prospective pass.

Shaw recrossed Howse Pass with his men, but snow began to fall and was soon piled four feet deep. One morning an avalanche swept down while the crew was departing for work. Shaw had foreseen the likelihood, and had made it a practice to cache supplies away from camp. The avalanche heaped debris several hundred feet deep, blocking the narrow valley. Their tents were destroyed, but Shaw and his men had blankets and food enough for the 65-mile forced march back to the railhead at Laggan (now Lake Louise), which they began that afternoon. When they arrived five days later, Shaw described his companions as looking like "wild men," their bootless feet wrapped in gunnysacks and deer hides. At the railroad's mess house they ate their first "civilized meal" in many months. So ended a routine season of surveying for the CPR.

A single avalanche had killed any hope for the Howse Pass route. The CPR was out of time. The following summer, the railway would lay track across Kicking Horse Pass, although no one believed that the route could be any better.

Chapter 1
The Pipedream of Millington Henry Synge

Canadian Confederation was more than 15 years away when an Irish soldier, a Royal Engineer named Millington Henry Synge, floated his idea. In January 1852, Synge presented a paper to the Royal Geographical Society in London: *Proposal for a Rapid Communication with the Pacific and the East, via British North America.* In it, the engineer described a transportation system — a hybrid of railways and canals — that would stretch from the Gulf of St. Lawrence to the Pacific Ocean.

In making his pitch in the stuffy chambers of the Society, Synge cared not for the possible future of a nation, the kernel of which was just beginning to coalesce. He had in mind the economic interests of the British Empire. With the disappearance five years earlier of Captain John Franklin's fourth expedition, British mariners and merchants had all but given up on a navigable Northwest Passage. The commercial fleets of the Netherlands, Spain, and Portugal, by nature of their slight geographical advantages, had long ruled the trade routes around the Cape of Good Hope to what were then called the East Indies. By nature of this maritime supremacy, those countries had also dominated the commercial and colonial interests of the Far East for more than two centuries.

The Northwest Passage was a bust, but Synge still believed that he could help forge a trade shortcut that would allow Britain to dominate world commerce. Although two centuries of fur trade experience in the wilds of British North America (as Canada was then known) had proven the landscape harsh, complex, and exacting, Synge thought it would be a simple task to build a transportation network across the middle latitudes of the continent. With ocean ports at each terminus, the plan would cleave some 3700 miles from what was then the shortest, strictly maritime route between Britain and its newest colonial interest, Australia.

Synge's scant knowledge of British North America stemmed from a brief military posting at Bytown, now Ottawa. In his paper he relied heavily on the published accounts of others — principally, fur trade explorers and governors. Synge was selective in what he included. His proposal brimmed with descriptions of park-like landscapes dotted with sylvan lakes, of luxuriant forests, of productive farmland that never needed to be left fallow, of mountains that were beautiful and inspiring, yet always — when it came to proposed transportation routes — trivial obstacles.

Synge penned an utterly fanciful description of the continental divide that separates the North Saskatchewan and Columbia river systems in the Rocky Mountains: "The width and elevation of the land of the dividing ridges are so slight, that in seasons of flood, the waters of these different systems commingle at their sources." The only place that such a flood had occurred since the end of the last ice age was in Synge's imagination.

What he included may have bent the truth, but what Synge excluded amounted to an outright lie. The six-month Canadian winters were merely an impediment to travel, not a crucible of existence. Summers were blissful, with not a mosquito, black fly, noseeum or horsefly to be found. First Peoples were background objects, with no claims, no rights, and posing no threat. The Gulf of St. Lawrence, the Great Lakes basin, the Canadian Shield, the prairies, the Rocky Mountains, and the five ranges of peaks that lay to their west — all of these, if Synge were to be believed, formed a straight shot for a railway and its attendant canal system. Synge described the Grand Rapid at the mouth of the Saskatchewan River — a three-mile long cataract whose banks were littered with the graves of drowned fur traders — as a "small obstacle." The "removal" of the rapid would enable navigation "to the very foot of the Rocky

Mountains, and in effect carry the Atlantic seaboard to their base." Synge's transcontinental route would breach the Rockies by an artificial waterway, constructed of "steps of still water."

When Synge put his thoughts to paper, Great Britain and most of Europe were at the height of a railway boom that had thoroughly transformed the way of life. From the mid-1700s to 1800, European commerce moved at the pace of a barge towed by mules. Beginning in 1804, British canals were supplanted by railways, the speed of whose locomotives began to impel industry and the pace of everyday affairs with the urgency of chugging steam. On the seas, too, transformation was underway, as freighters driven by steam-powered turbines overtook the clippers, barques, and galleons of sail.

Although there were 9000 miles of railway track in the U.S. in 1850, the steam era was much slower in coming to British North America, where only 222 miles of track had been laid when Synge proposed his plan. But because there was a perceived inevitability to the construction of railways everywhere in the world, Synge's idea, although it seems far-fetched today, caught the interest of British newspapers.

Synge was not the only railway dreamer of his time. An Englishman, Robert Carmichael Smyth — another soldier and engineer — proposed a similar scheme. The principal difference was the source of construction labour. Synge favoured importing the unemployed from Britain; Smyth thought that convicts could build the railway in the frozen wilds — his version of a colonial Siberia.

Both proposals included maps with bold lines showing "the routes of communication" between the Atlantic and the Pacific oceans across 3600 miles of Canada. Those lines fell eerily close to the eventual route of Canada's first transcontinental railway, the Canadian Pacific. But beyond the obvious impediments of landscape, labour, and capital, neither plan mentioned what was at the time the greatest obstacle — the Hudson's Bay Company (HBC).

By nature of a Royal Charter granted in 1666, the HBC owned a subcontinent known as Rupert's Land — all territory that drained into Hudson Bay. For almost two centuries it had been HBC policy to drive off rival fur traders and to stifle settlement. To discourage interlopers, the HBC tore out bridges wherever they were built. Not a single span existed across a lake or river in central British North America, west of Sault Ste. Marie. To imagine that the HBC would be willing to grant easements for a transcontinental railway was the pipedream of engineers.

Interest might have then foundered if left solely to the British newspapers, but it was sustained on two fronts. In 1848, a young Irishman named John Palliser returned to Britain from a hunting trip along the Missouri River in the U.S. Midwest. Palliser began to fancy himself an explorer, but he had a problem: he had been raised in a family of means but was now short of cash. He approached the Royal Geographical Society to sponsor a quest to chart the lands of central and western British North America. The Society was keen. In 1856, it commissioned the North West America Exploring Expedition, sending it overseas under Palliser's command the following year. The expedition had many goals, but among them was to inventory potential railway routes through the Canadian Rockies.

In his summary report, Palliser was utterly skeptical about the possibility of constructing a transcontinental railway entirely on Canadian soil. He described the Canadian Shield, the billion-year-old granitic soul of central Canada and the most ancient geological feature on the surface of the planet, as "...*the* obstacle of the country... almost beyond the remedies of art." Palliser considered the southern prairies worthless to agriculture, whereas he described a fertile belt to the north in the valley of the North Saskatchewan River. For the next 20 years, the net effect of Palliser's appraisal was to deter British investors from any interest in a Canadian transcontinental railway.

Palliser was still writing his report in London when a Canadian Scot weighed in on the discussion. In 1862, Sandford Fleming, a surveyor and railroad construction engineer, published a paper, *Observations and Practical Suggestions on the Subject of a Railway through British North America.* It was a meticulously researched work, long on detail, short on assumptions. Finally, the politicians, the press, and the public could consider the proposition on the basis of a no-nonsense document written by a proven railway builder.

Fleming's paper was but one domino that fell between 1858 and 1871, when events propelled the idea of a Canadian transcontinental railway from parlour room discussion to political debate. The Cariboo gold rush of 1858 attracted thousands to the colony of British Columbia (BC). Almost all arrived by steamship from San Francisco, underscoring the need for an overland route from the east. The American Civil War of 1861-63 raised the issue of border security between the U.S. and British North America. After the war, the U.S. possessed a large, idle standing army. Many Americans, including Secretary of State William H. Seward, advocated Manifest Destiny. They spoke openly of using force to appropriate British territory to "finish the job" begun in the American Revolution. There was ample precedent to fear U.S. sabre rattling; the Americans had annexed Texas and California in 1847. The U.S. Midwest was beginning to fill with settlers, whereas, due to the HBC, there were only 23,000 Europeans in British territory west of Lake Superior, most of them on Vancouver Island. Railway building had become an obsession. In a decade, track length in the U.S. had more than tripled to 31,000 miles; in Canada it had increased almost tenfold to 2138 miles.

In 1867, Seward purchased Alaska from Russia, stating that "nature had intended the whole of the continent to be American." BC began to feel the squeeze between two arms of U.S. territory: the Alaska panhandle of "Seward's Icebox" to the north and that part of the Oregon Territory (later to be Washington state) to the south. In the same year, Ontario, Quebec, New Brunswick, and Nova Scotia entered Canadian Confederation. Two years later, the Hudson's Bay Company ceded Rupert's Land to the fledgling country.

The final domino that made construction of a transcontinental railway inevitable fell in 1871, when Canada's first Prime Minister, John A. Macdonald, struck the bargain with BC that ushered the anxious colony into Canada. What tipped the scale was Macdonald's promise to begin construction of a railway to BC within two years and to complete the project within ten years. Synge's pipedream had become a political platform.

Although Macdonald's plan had critics aplenty, political and public will were in favour. The only impediment that remained was, as Sandford Fleming had put it in 1862, "half a continent [that had] to be redeemed and parted at least from a wild state of nature." Fleming had done such a splendid job with his proposal that John A. Macdonald appointed him to survey the route for the railway and to oversee its construction.

Chapter 2
Ocean to Ocean

S andford Fleming, Engineer-in-Chief of the Pacific Railway, knew a thing or two about railroads. At the time of his appointment in April 1871, he was 45 and was in charge of surveying and constructing the Intercolonial Railway, which would link Canada's four eastern provinces. Construction of the Intercolonial dragged on until 1876, so for the first five years of his tenure with the Pacific Railway, Fleming faced the monumental task of overseeing railway construction from coast to coast.

In March 1871, the government established the Pacific Survey to find a route that would link existing railway lines in eastern Canada with BC. Fleming divided the country west from Ottawa into 21 sections, assigning to each a survey party

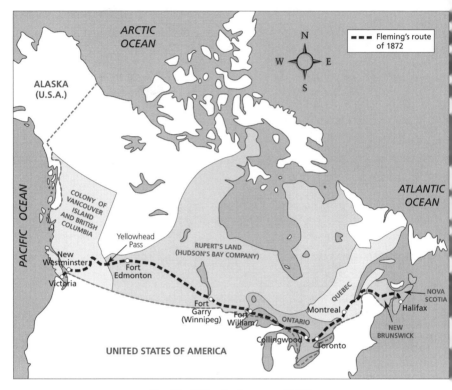

Sandford Fleming's route of 1872

of 40 men. Although other terrain would ultimately present more problems, Fleming's initial concern involved where the rails would cross the Rocky Mountains. He assigned surveyor Walter Moberly to scout Howse Pass in the central Rockies. After Fleming digested Moberly's preliminary reports, he dismissed Howse Pass in favour of Yellowhead Pass. In April 1872 the government committed to building the railway by that route although the rails would cross the prairies some 250 miles north of the U.S. border — far enough away that U.S. branch lines might have been able to infiltrate future Canadian soil.

Fleming had never travelled west of Georgian Bay. His remedy for this knowledge gap was typical of the man. With the route for the railway decided — at least in his mind — he crossed the country to inspect the terrain and to meet with surveying parties. As companions, Fleming chose his son, Franky, and George Munro Grant, a Presbyterian minister from Halifax. The three men journeyed separately by rail from Halifax to Toronto, where they met on July 15, 1872. The following day, they took passage from Toronto to rail's end at Collingwood, where they boarded a steamship for Fort William (now Thunder Bay). They bypassed the rugged north shore of Lake Superior, which, had Fleming been travelling on foot, would have given him pause.

On the ship, Fleming met botanist John Macoun, a college professor on a summer collecting trip. Macoun accepted Fleming's invitation to join the group. At Fort William, the expedition transferred to wagon, and then to canoe along the old fur trade route to Fort Garry (now Winnipeg). Charles Horetzky joined the party for the trip by horse and cart across the prairies to Fort Edmonton. Horetzky, an unemployed photographer, was a friend of Charles Tupper, a member of John A. Macdonald's cabinet. This was Fleming's first taste of the cronyism that would dog his tenure as Engineer-in-Chief.

At Fort Edmonton the party split. Fleming instructed Macoun and Horetzky to head northwest, where they eventually crossed the Rockies at Pine Pass. Fleming and Grant continued west, crossing the Rockies on foot with packhorses. They carried on to Kamloops and then to Burrard Inlet (now Vancouver), a proposed terminus for the railway. There the pair boarded a steamer and inspected Bute Inlet, another possible railway terminus. When they disembarked at Victoria on Vancouver Island a week later, they had covered 5314 miles in 103 days, using seven modes of travel.

Each evening, Grant had documented the journey, on occasion resorting to making notes on birchbark. From his journal, he created the book, *Ocean to Ocean* — the first Canadian travel narrative written after Confederation. Grant composed wonderful descriptions of the Canadian west before it was transformed by broad-axe, railway steel, and plough. To him, the journey was a breeze: "None of us suffered from Indians, wild beasts, the weather, or any of the hardships incidental to travel in a new and lone land." Grant extolled the virtues of Yellowhead Pass for railway construction: "Instead of contracted canyon or savage torrent raging among beetling precipices as we had feared, the Pass is really a pleasant open meadow. So easy an ingress into the heart of the Rocky Mountains... could hardly have been hoped for."

Given that he did not walk it, Grant's description of the country north of Lake Superior was a lie: "We are satisfied that the rugged and hitherto unknown country extending from the Upper Ottawa [River] to the Red River of the North [Manitoba], is not, as it has always been represented on maps executed by our [American] neighbours and copied by ourselves, impracticable for a railway; but entirely the reverse."

Ocean to Ocean was a best-seller. But, as with everything connected with the Pacific Railway, the book spawned controversy when newspapers discovered that Fleming had appropriated government funds to pay the printing costs.

Fleming's trip cemented Yellowhead Pass as his choice for the route through the Rockies. But it was not to be. The fickle political winds that blew throughout the planning and the construction of the Pacific Railway eventually brewed into a tempest that toppled him from favour. Yellowhead Pass would not echo with the whistle of locomotive steam until the construction of the Grand Trunk Pacific and the Canadian Northern railways, almost 40 years later.

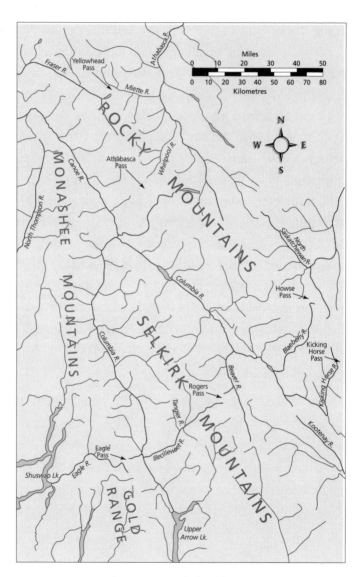

The mountains before the CPR

Chapter 3
The World According to Walter J. Moberly

In any great enterprise, there are those in the right place at the right time. History celebrates them, sometimes assigning a rank and an importance that exceeds their contribution. There are also individuals who labour greatly in the service of a cause, only to be thwarted when it comes to recognition. Sometimes, others conspire to defame them; sometimes they denigrate themselves. In his lifetime, Walter J. Moberly attained stature as a surveyor, as a promoter of roads and railways, and as a public servant. Yet, conflicts and frequent falls from grace marred his accomplishments. As a result, history has largely forgotten the man who, for 20 years, was the greatest private promoter of a Canadian transcontinental railway and the most prolific traveller of Canadian wilderness.

Moberly began his surveying career at age 20 in 1852, when he hired on for the construction of the Ontario, Simcoe, and Huron Railway. For three years, he served under Sandford Fleming. It was the first of many times that their paths would cross. Moberly reported that the two men got along well during this time.

In 1854, Moberly sought to combine his love of undeveloped country with his ethic for hard work. He purchased timber leases along the north shores of Lake Huron and Lake Superior — areas accessible only by boat. The following year, Moberly quit his railway job. For three summers, he explored the rugged country of north-central Ontario. In the off-seasons, he pursued politicians, to whom he pitched his dream. It was the era of "pamphleteering," when anyone with a vibrant idea and a few dollars to spare papered the streets to let everyone know. Moberly's aims were to plot the line for a railroad from Ontario to what is now Manitoba, and to muster support for its construction.

In 1858, Moberly heard of the Palliser Expedition. Envious of the well-financed British group, he decided that he must meet John Palliser at the western end of his journey to learn about potential routes for a transcontinental railway. Moberly would then take that information to James Douglas, Governor of Vancouver Island and British Columbia. Moberly assumed that Douglas would commission him to survey the route for a railway that would link those colonies to eastern Canada.

With no prior notice to those on the west coast on whom his plan depended, Moberly sold his interests. Although he arrived in Victoria broke and without possessions, having been robbed during the trip around Cape Horn, the surveyor wasted no time in presenting himself to Governor Douglas just before Christmas. From Douglas, Moberly learned that Palliser was not due to arrive for almost another year. Moberly covered his disappointment, proclaiming that he "was going to set out to try and find a line through the mountains suitable to build a railway." Governor Douglas was astonished. Not only did this newcomer know nothing about the country that he intended to traverse, he proposed to make his first acquaintance with it in winter.

Moberly's first foray into the wilds of what would later become BC ended predictably. He followed trails beaten by gold-seekers, but got no further than Lillooet. He prospected nearby, ran out of food and money, and retreated to free grub at the HBC post of Fort Langley. The journey should have been an embarrassment. But Moberly spun it into something of a success by reporting to Governor Douglas on the need to upgrade the miners' trails into a network of wagon roads — a proposal to which the governor promptly committed funds.

Late in 1859, Moberly met John Palliser, who "reported that it was not possible to get a practical line for a railway through the mountains of British Columbia." After reviewing

Palliser's assessment, Governor Douglas abandoned the idea of a railway link to eastern Canada.

For the next four years, Moberly held contracts to build wagon roads in southern BC. Late in 1864, he became Assistant Surveyor General of the colony. His first assignment was to plot a road and railway route through the area drained by the Columbia River. Moberly soon made the discovery that embodied the contradictions of his career. It would be his claim to fame, a partial cause of his professional demise, and the seed of the bitterness that marred his later years. At the mouth of a river on the southern arm of Shuswap Lake, near present day Sicamous, Moberly disturbed a pair of bald eagles by attempting to shoot the nest out from under them. The birds took flight, following the river eastward from the lake. In an account written 20 years later, Moberly made a self-serving observation: "I knew that eagles always follow along a stream or make for an opening in the mountains. It struck me that if I followed them, I might find the much wished-for pass."

Moberly never did follow the eagles, but a few weeks later he found himself near the site of present day Revelstoke on the Columbia River. He thought that he might be east of the valley up which the eagles had flown. To test this theory, Moberly and his men climbed a peak on the west side of the Columbia Valley. The ascent took two days. From the summit, Moberly gazed down on the mother lode of his surveying dreams. To the west, he could see Shuswap Lake. The valley into which the eagles had flown wound toward him to end in a pass at the foot of his peak. A lake occupied the pass. From it a stream flowed east into the Columbia River. The gradients were gentle, the distance was short; and the elevation of the pass (later measured at 1841 feet) was low. Walter Moberly had discovered the chink in the armor of the Monashee Mountains.

Although it was desirable that he also establish routes at the same latitude through the Selkirk Mountains and the Rocky Mountains, Moberly knew that the old fur trade route circumvented the Selkirks by following the Columbia River north to Big Bend. From there, river and trail routes led to two passes across the Rockies: Athabasca Pass and Howse Pass. He had not travelled either, but Moberly was confident that one or the other would work for a railway. In discovering Eagle Pass, Walter Moberly had, as he would soon tell anyone who might listen, solved the problem of where to locate a railway line across BC and, by implication, across what would soon become Canada.

Later in the season, Moberly attempted to find a pass across the Selkirk Mountains by exploring along the Illecillewaet River. Where the river forked, near the present day western boundary of Glacier National Park, he followed the northerly branch (now called Tangier River) to a dead end. Winter came early and the surveyor could not entice his men — who had been dining on dried squirrel meat — to continue. Moberly characterized the southeast branch of the river as "... the one that, judging from its general bearing, would be most likely to afford a pass in the direction wished for."

He was right in that assessment, but would never benefit from it. The following year, Moberly sent his assistant, Albert Perry, to explore the pass at the head of the southeast fork. Perry, whose nickname was "The Mountaineer," met his match in the Illecillewaet River valley. When he returned it was to tell his boss that he had not reached the pass. Moberly lamented in his journal: "... his failure is a great disappointment to me."

Disappointment mounted when BC Governor James Seymour abandoned the idea of an overland link to eastern Canada. Moberly quit his government job and spent the next four years in the western U.S. At the time of Confederation, he was in charge of a warehouse in San Francisco. Later, he hung his shingle as a civil surveyor and mined silver in Nevada. While abroad, he clung to the dream that Canada would soon build a great railway and that the politicians would defer to him for his knowledge of the best route.

A telegram making just such a request came in June 1871. At an Ottawa meeting, John A. Macdonald and Sandford Fleming commissioned Moberly to head the BC operations of the Pacific Survey. Moberly made for Howse Pass, which he crossed with relative ease. The surveyor was so convinced of the Howse Pass route, he did not wait for instructions for the 1872 season. Instead, he let contracts for supplies and hired additional men to make a full location survey.

Moberly was set to depart Victoria for the field in April 1872 on an early morning steamer. In the middle of the night the Lieutenant-Governor of BC summoned him and handed over a telegram from Sandford Fleming. The Engineer-in-Chief dropped an anvil onto Moberly's dreams by telling him that the Pacific Railway would cross the Rockies at Yellowhead Pass.

Moberly was not only crushed emotionally and professionally, he was in a tremendous pickle financially. As Fleming had not authorized any of the preparations for the 1872 season, the surveyor feared that he would be liable for the costs. Pack trains were already freighting supplies into the field.

Moberly set off in a panic on a crazy course through Oregon and BC, attempting to overtake the packers, buy them out of their contracts, and redirect them before they learned of his predicament and jacked their rates. He was largely successful, but many supplies had already been delivered to depots where they would never be used — $7000 worth was abandoned at Eagle Pass. When Fleming later saw Moberly's accounting, he complained: "It seemed to me as if some country store had been bought out..."

In September, Moberly trudged through what is now Jasper National Park, looking for his boss. Fleming and George Munro Grant were two months into their *Ocean to Ocean* journey when he met them near Yellowhead Pass. According to Moberly, the encounter was strained. Soon after Fleming moved on, Moberly received a letter telling him that he had been replaced. "This was joyful news for me, for I saw the way clear to get out of the distasteful occupation of making useless surveys."

Moberly and Fleming had one more meeting, this time in Ottawa, where Moberly was "very coldly received." The mutual litanies of complaint mounted higher. Fleming detained Moberly for two months for an audit, but paid the surveyor nothing for his time or expenses. The passing of the years only made Moberly more resentful. In his written accounts, he referred to Fleming only by title — and that spelled in lower case. In Moberly's last description of his professional life, written in 1909, he chose to contradict information included in his original reports. He claimed that Albert Perry had reached Rogers Pass in 1866, and thus to Perry — and by implication, to Moberly — should have gone the credit of determining the line of the CPR through the Selkirk Mountains and the Monashee Mountains.

In both the short view and the long view of history, when self-promotion becomes fabrication, those who pen the lies fall from favour. This has been Walter Moberly's fate. However, not all of his self-promotion was off the mark. In 1909, he wrote an accurate précis of his place: "It is very gratifying to me that my exertions, extending over a period of nearly a quarter of a century tended very materially to insure the welfare and prosperity of many thousands of people throughout British Columbia, as well as through the country extending from the Rocky Mountains to Winnipeg." For this, for his discovery of Eagle Pass, and for his tireless exploration, Walter Moberly deserves to be better known.

34

Chapter 4
Two Streaks of Rust

The construction of Canada's first transcontinental railway was a knock-down, drag-out battle on all fronts that lasted more than 14 years. While the surveyors stumbled through muskeg, hacked rights of way through forest and shintangle, and passed frigid winters in remote camps, the politicians at the helm took pieces off each other for every conceivable reason.

The early political landscape of Canada held two camps partitioned by invective: John A. Macdonald's Conservatives and Alexander Mackenzie's Liberals. Macdonald was a powerhouse, a man of vision and intellect, who dreamed big and drank heavily. His counterpart, Mackenzie, was a stone-faced puritan, disinclined to imagine a country beyond the four

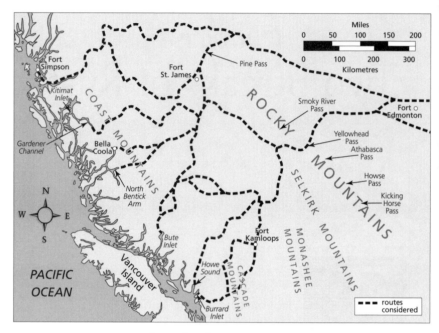

One railroad, too many routes

existing provinces of eastern Canada. These two political figures and their colleagues went at it in words and letters, both publicly and in the protection of the House of Commons, in a manner that would be considered scandalous today.

Macdonald was on record as stating that the Pacific Railway "must be taken up by a body of capitalists and not constructed by the government directly." But in its first incarnation, his dream of transcontinental steel was the opposite — a purely political venture. Macdonald was compelled to reverse his view by the urgent need to settle the prairies.

One newspaper had put the issue succinctly: "With the construction of the railway, the country will be populated by Canadians; without it by Americans."

Canada was home to scarcely three million people of European descent in 1871. Less than 30,000 lived west of Lake Superior. Cursory estimates of the survey and construction costs of the railway tallied almost $100 million. Given that the government was also bankrolling other railway lines in eastern Canada, Mackenzie's Liberals were right to characterize as "reckless" and as "insanity" Macdonald's promise to complete a transcontinental railway by 1881. Edward Blake, a prominent Liberal, predicted that Macdonald's dream, if ever built, would soon be nothing more than "two streaks of rust in the wilderness."

Between 1871 and 1877, crews of the Pacific Survey tracked through 46,000 miles of Canadian wilderness. Axemen cleared prospective grades and surveyors took measurements along more than a quarter of that distance. The surveyors marked routes with more than 600,000 wooden stakes and 25,000 benchmarks. But the wild country did not yield easily to their labour — 38 men died. They drowned in rivers and lakes — tossed from leaky canoes whose cracks they had stuffed with mud and leaves — or pitched into rapids from makeshift rafts. They plunged through ice. They were killed by kicks from horses or were crushed by falling trees. Others perished in forest fires or withered, half-mad from scurvy. Some froze to death, others were killed by grizzly bears. Violence between workers was common but, surprisingly, the death toll did not record murder.

While the Liberals and the Conservatives bickered in the comfort of the House of Commons, surveyors gave their lives as pawns, sacrificed to the exploration of routes that were unfeasible, mere political whims, or both. There was some discussion as to the route that the rails should take across the prairies, but that debate paled compared to the squabbling about the route through the Rockies and across BC. Because there were so many egos, minds, cities, businessmen, and political views to appease in the mix, the politicians directed the surveying crews to plot almost 30 variations west of the Rockies.

A principal reason for this squandering of men, money, and time was disagreement over the western terminus of the railway, which — and here for once all the politicians agreed — would become a major city. So surveyors explored routes to Burrard Inlet (now the site of Vancouver), Esquimault (adjacent to Victoria), Bute Inlet, Kitimat, the Gardner Channel, Bella Coola, North Bentick Arm, Howe Sound, and Fort Simpson. Even after Fleming's selection of Yellowhead Pass, many of these locations remained under consideration, with multiple approaches surveyed to them.

Macdonald's government resigned in 1873 as a result of the "Pacific Scandal," when it became known that the Prime Minister had accepted a $350,000 political donation from Montreal financier and shipping mogul, Hugh Allan. In return, Macdonald had given Allan's consortium the Pacific Railway construction contract and access to a 50-million-acre land grant. Allan and Macdonald passionately attempted to argue their way out of the mess, but the paper trail was damning. The electorate voted the Liberals to power in the ensuing election. Macdonald barely escaped going to jail.

Among his government's last acts, Macdonald chose Bute Inlet as the route to tidewater in BC and directed crews to turn sod for the "western terminus" of the railway at Esquimalt on Vancouver Island. He did this to satisfy voters in Victoria. But Macdonald made the gestures as if living in a bubble, oblivious that his proposed route required almost ten miles of tunnels along Bute Inlet alone and a 29-mile crossing of the Strait of Georgia that necessitated many bridges, two of which would have been longer than any in the world.

Mackenzie took office in January 1874, inheriting a railway that he did not support — with what he called its "appalling obligations" of money and resources — and federal coffers devoid of the necessary funds. But the railway had been pledged to BC and, at least in appearances, its construction was underway.

To his credit, Mackenzie did lay the first track of the Pacific Railway in 1875. But the location — west of Lake Superior — revealed the new Prime Minister's lack of commitment. He planned to make a connection to existing lines in the east not by rail, but by using steamers on the Great Lakes. He even considered employing steamboats on the North

Saskatchewan River all the way to the Rockies, despite being advised that freeze-up and seasonal low water would have kept such a route unnavigable for six months each year.

More so than the mountains of western Canada, the 467 miles from Lake Superior to Winnipeg almost became the undoing of the Pacific Railway. The approach to the surveying and construction created a legacy of problems — technical, political, and financial. Fleming's surveyor on the section, Henry Carre, plotted the route in winter. By using dogsleds and snowshoes, Carre's men travelled with greater ease than they would have in summer, but the tactic was penny-wise and pound-foolish. Carre did not see how much of the country was muskeg and how little fill was available for embankments and footings. He later commented: "If the profile showed a practicable line, then I was satisfied. I never went back over it again...." The next people to see the country were the contractors and their workers, slogging through peat-choked muck in the bug-filled hell of summer.

Fleming's department let the first construction contracts in a hodgepodge fashion, in a process rife with bribery and patronage. The contractors required nitroglycerine and fill in quantities so enormous that their low-ball bids soon went bankrupt. Mackenzie fished half-heartedly for private investors, offering cash and land subsidies but with no takers in the dim economic climate of the day. The Prime Minister despaired, stating that BC could never be linked to the rest of Canada by rail as soon as 1881 — not "with all the power of men and all the money in the empire." This prompted mumblings of secession from BC. As if to put a personal stamp on the chaos, Mackenzie changed the western terminus, choosing Burrard Inlet, an act that pitched the Victorians against the soon-to-be Vancouverites. Meanwhile, Fleming, exhausted from his work on the Intercolonial and the Pacific railways, booked off on a year-long medical leave.

Fed up with the muddling, the public returned Macdonald to power in December 1878. Central to Macdonald's successful campaign was his three-pronged National Policy: enacting a trade tariff to protect Canadian commerce, reaffirming the promise of a railway to BC, and encouraging settlement in the west. Macdonald directed Fleming to make a new start on the railway. Within a year, the Engineer-in-Chief had awarded four construction contracts in BC. Anybody could have been forgiven for expecting that the flip-flopping on routes was over. But completion of the Pacific Survey alone would take another three years.

To help put the Pacific Railway back on track, Macdonald appointed a Royal Commission to tell the country why, after nine years, scarcely 100 miles of rails had been laid. Seeing the tempest coming to a head, Fleming resigned in May 1880 before the commission took evidence. Nonetheless, the final report marked him as the scapegoat.

Fleming later made a submission to Parliament: "A reader of the Report of the Commission without knowledge of the facts, could only come to one conclusion... that three successive Administrations had employed a man [Fleming] to conduct the heaviest works ever undertaken in Canada, whose one aim and object was to do everything the way in which it should not be done."

In late June, the Prime Minister proclaimed that three groups of financiers were interested in constructing the Pacific Railway. Macdonald and his Minister of Railways and Canals, Charles Tupper, sailed to England to begin the negotiations. Two parties dropped out of the bidding, but Macdonald completed a preliminary agreement with the third party in September 1880. The Pacific Railway was about to shift from political enterprise to private venture. But which route would it follow?

Chapter 5

The Bishop, the General, and the Impossible

I f John A. Macdonald had employed a political publicist in 1880, the Prime Minister's return from London would have been a dream come true. Standing on the rear steps of a railway car — the perfect pulpit — Macdonald proclaimed to an excited Montreal throng that he had secured private backing for the Pacific Railway. A consortium of Canadian, American, British, French, and German financiers — soon to be known as the Syndicate — would put up the money; Canada would be united by railway steel.

There was truth in the broad sweep of Macdonald's announcement, but the absence of details concealed many surprises. When the contract with the Syndicate became

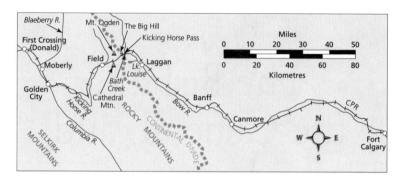

Kicking Horse Pass

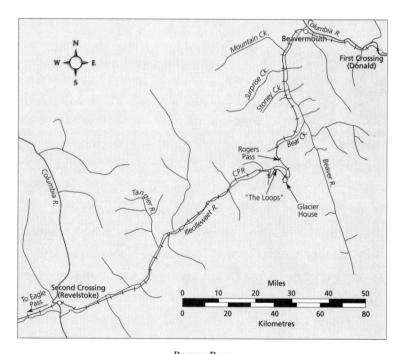

Rogers Pass

public, Canadian newspapers and the electorate reeled from the particulars. Macdonald's government had agreed to pay the $37-million cost of the surveys and to give the Syndicate $25 million of taxpayers' cash along with 25 million acres of land, which the Syndicate could sell for one dollar an acre. The Syndicate would pay no taxes on unsold land for 20 years, nor on materials used in the railway's construction. Land used for railway operations would be tax-exempt forever. The Syndicate would be given title to all publicly constructed segments intended to be part of the transcontinental route as they were completed. These included two of the more difficult sections that had been bleeding government coffers for five years: the Canadian Shield and the Fraser Canyon. The government warranted that, for 20 years, no competing railway would be constructed south of the Syndicate's line or run within 15 miles of the U.S. border. In return, the Syndicate promised to complete the railway from coast to coast on Canadian soil within ten years.

Debate raged in the newspapers, on the street, and in Parliament, but the Pacific Railway bill chugged through the House of Commons and the Senate to receive royal assent on February 15, 1881. The next day, the Canadian Pacific Railway Company (CPR) incorporated to begin the monumental business of fulfilling its obligation.

The executive of the CPR included James Jerome Hill of St. Paul, Minnesota. Hill headed steamship lines, supply companies, coal mines, and U.S. railways. Although Canadian born of Irish descent, Hill epitomized the canny Yankee capitalist — when he died, his net worth was estimated at $60 million. Hill was so pro-American, he celebrated the signing of the Syndicate's contract by becoming a U.S. citizen. He was the only Syndicate member with railway experience. To the eternal vexation of Canadian newspapers, in the early days of the CPR, whenever Hill needed something done, he hired an American.

The first Yankee that Hill added to the payroll was Major Albert Bowman Rogers, a 52- year-old engineer who had earned a reputation in the U.S. Midwest as "The Railway Pathfinder." Hill instructed Rogers to survey four passes in the Rockies. Only the more northerly of these — Howse Pass — was known. As part of the transcontinental route, the CPR would be inheriting railway lines built by the government. The gap between these lines extended from Winnipeg to near Fort Kamloops, BC. Hill and the CPR executive were beginning to realize that a more southerly route between those points would be significantly shorter, less expensive to construct, finished sooner, and better able to fend off competition from U.S. railways.

Hill had also been influenced by the published opinion of John Macoun, the hitch-hiking botanist who had joined Sandford Fleming's expedition in 1872. In blunt contrast to the view of John Palliser, Macoun considered the southern prairies prime for agriculture. Climatologists now know that the 19th century was the wettest in western Canada in the past 2000 years. As the Dirty Thirties and more recent droughts have demonstrated, Palliser's appraisal was accurate. But the Syndicate embraced Macoun's assessment because it told them what they wanted to hear. Hill also knew that squatters and speculators had already staked the Yellowhead Pass route. A more southerly line, built quickly, would preclude the necessity of buying people out.

In addition to plotting a route through the Rockies, Hill directed Rogers to find a pass through the Selkirk Mountains. If successful, Hill promised to name the pass for Rogers and to reward the surveyor with a gold watch and a cheque for $5000.

If a novelist today created the character of Major Rogers, the writer might be accused of going "over the top." Unlike many in the continent's railway surveying corps, Rogers had been schooled as an engineer, with a degree from Yale. But in appearance, Rogers was as far removed from the typical Yale graduate as could be imagined. He was short and wiry, with an outlandish mustache. He possessed a sharp tongue, and a penchant for hurling expletives that earned him more nicknames: The Bishop and Hell's Bells Rogers. Tobacco juice repeatedly spurted from his mouth, adding emphasis to his commentary — sometimes well aimed and well timed — but usually not. Rogers dressed like a derelict. But if anyone doubted his ability to travel the wilderness, they reconsidered after trying to keep up with him.

Rogers had become a major when commissioned during the Dakota Sioux uprising in 1862. His subsequent career was proof that a title alone does not make a good leader. He was cursed with a dangerous combination of drive and ruthlessness. Men feared him for his temper, for his overbearing demeanor, and for the manner in which he consistently under-provisioned his explorations. He could travel on a diet of raw beans, bacon, and chewing tobacco, and expected others to do likewise.

At the end of one season, Rogers and his crew descended on the camp of fellow surveyor, J.H. Secretan, who described Rogers as a "ruffian," and his men as "scarecrows." Although Secretan extended every hospitality, Rogers complained about the treatment, reporting to the chief engineer that Secretan was "living like the Czar of Russia and would absolutely ruin any Railway Corporation in the world." According to Rogers, Secretan had "Brussels carpets" in his tents and dined on turkeys and geese. The carpets were burlap and the fowl were wild birds that Secretan had shot.

Rogers' first exploration, in late April 1881, took him to the west slope of the Selkirk Mountains. He mustered a party at Fort Kamloops and crossed the Monashee Mountains (using Walter Moberly's Eagle Pass) to gain the Columbia River at the present site of Revelstoke. As Albert Perry had done 15 years earlier — and likely no one had done since — Rogers and his men plunged eastward into the wild valley of the Illecillewaet River. Hampered by hundred pound packs, the thigh-deep porridge of the late-spring snowpack, and the unfulfilled expectation that the men would secure rations by hunting while on the move, the dozen men eventually stumbled onto the crest of a pass. Rogers' nephew Albert, part of the crew, later remarked of that uphill journey: "Many a time I wished myself dead."

The pass puzzled Rogers. It was not oriented east-west as he had expected, but north-south. The Major ordered his men to ascend a ridge so that they could better reconnoitre the land. The all-day climb provided an aerial view of a parallel valley to the east, which, Rogers surmised, received a stream that flowed from the new pass. If the valley led to the Columbia River, the surveyor had discovered a route through the Selkirks. Typically, Rogers had not requisitioned enough food to carry on. He would later learn that his party had been only 18 miles from the upper reach of the Columbia River. In saving a few dollars, Rogers had wasted part of a season. After a freezing night on the ridge, the men descended to the Illecillewaet River. With rumbling stomachs, they retreated west.

Rogers next stopped on the eastern slope of the Rockies, where he located a line through the Bow Valley to the eastern entrance of Kicking Horse Pass. Near the pass, Rogers nearly paid a dear price for his temper. On horseback, Rogers and packer Tom Wilson came to the edge of a turbulent glacial stream. Wilson suggested that they camp on the near bank and cross in the morning, when the stream's volume would have dropped.

"Afraid of it are you? Want the old man to show you how

to ford it?" And with that, the Major drove his steed into the frigid stream. The water bowled the horse over in an instant. Wilson was obliged to rescue Rogers, whose temper had understandably cooled. The horse made its way out of the creek, fortunately on the near bank. The incident provided a name for the tributary — Bath Creek.

At the end of the 1881 season, the CPR executive summoned Rogers to Montreal to make a report. The Major testified that the Kicking Horse-Selkirk route would work although he had not even set foot in the lower Kicking Horse Valley. The desperate executive took Rogers at his word and, in January 1882, stunned the country by announcing that the CPR would cross the Rockies by way of Kicking Horse Pass.

After fretting the winter away, Rogers took to the mountains too early in 1882. In May, the surveyor and five others attempted to cross the Selkirks from the east. A week into the journey they were starving, when the propitious discovery of an abandoned canoe allowed them to speed back to camp. After regrouping, Rogers embarked again on July 17. The going was only marginally better. For eight days his party toiled, following the Beaver River to Bear Creek (now Connaught Creek) and its sources in the Selkirks. Pestered by blackflies and mosquitoes, the men at times covered only two miles a day.

On July 24, Rogers gained the northern edge of the pass that he had reached the previous summer. He had breached the Selkirks. From that day, the clearing where he stood became known as Rogers Pass. With fame assured, the Major returned to the Rockies to complete the survey of Kicking Horse Pass and the intervening ground along the Columbia River.

Rogers had one nagging doubt, not about the feasibility of the Kicking Horse-Rogers Pass route, but that a better route might exist. No one had given Howse Pass serious consideration since Walter Moberly's survey in 1871. In the Bow Valley, Rogers recruited Tom Wilson for a reconnaissance. Deadfalls and swamps on the way to Bow Pass made travel on horseback tedious. After two days, Rogers grew impatient. Declaring that Wilson would be able to make the remainder of the trip in "ten days easy" and offering him a $50 bonus, Rogers enticed the young packer to carry on alone on foot. Wilson completed the trip, but it took 12 days and almost killed him. After Wilson recounted his ordeal, Rogers struck Howse Pass from consideration.

Although the route through the Bow Valley and over Howse Pass would have been 28 miles longer than the Kicking Horse Pass route, the grades on either side of Howse Pass were moderate by comparison. By making such a feeble effort to explore Howse Pass, Rogers helped commit the CPR to the greater perpetual expense and danger of operating the Kicking Horse Pass route.

By the end of 1882 Rogers had located a line through the Rockies and Selkirks that kept to the maximum grade allowed in the CPR's contract — 2.2 percent or 116 feet per mile. But the route was impractical. The first 18 miles of the line west from Kicking Horse Pass ran on a sidehill, avalanche-swept in its entirety. The section would have cost $124,000 per mile, and would have required many tunnels — two of them in succession totalling 1400 feet through Mt. Stephen.

In the Bow Valley between Calgary and present day Banff, Rogers' line amounted to the greatest surveying gaffe in Canadian railway history. He called for a mud tunnel half a mile long and on a curve, the crossing of 13 ravines — each averaging 400 feet long and 100 feet deep — and a half-mile long rock tunnel. James Ross, the chief construction engineer, characterized the line as a "nightmare" that "would hold us back a year." In March 1883, Ross invited surveyor Charles Shaw into his Winnipeg office to look over the profile and provide an opinion.

Shaw made a quick assessment. "I can get a far better line than that." There followed an explosive retort from across the office: "That's the best line that can be got through that country. Who the hell are you, anyway?" Without responding to Rogers, Shaw told Ross that he would resurvey the line west from Calgary to the mountain front, and "If I don't save at least half a million dollars... I won't ask [for] any pay for my season's work." Rogers shrieked and fumed, but Ross later took Shaw up on the offer.

Shaw delivered. His survey saved $1,350,000 dollars in just 55 miles, most of it by simply locating the line to the opposite bank of the Bow River. Ross assigned Shaw to resurvey the route all the way across Rogers Pass and to take a last-minute look at Howse Pass. Shaw continued to find problems. Near present day Banff, Rogers had plotted a tunnel through a small mountain. Shaw readily saw that the rails could be laid in the Bow Valley north of the mountain, saving a mile of track and two steep grades, not to mention the tunnel. The pack trail that Rogers had used many times went up, over, and down the mountain, providing a clear view of the easier alternative, but Rogers had failed to see it. Shaw characterized the proposed location as "the most extraordinary blunder I have ever known in the way of engineering." And so Tunnel Mountain was christened although the tunnel was never built.

In 1884, Rogers worked as a location engineer in the Selkirks and in the Monashee Mountains. But no one trusted him. The CPR dispatched an engineer to check up on his work, another engineer to appraise that assessment, and yet another engineer to give a last opinion. To finally put his mind at ease, William Cornelius Van Horne, General Manager of the CPR, had Rogers lead him on foot from west to east along the proposed route in BC. Travelling with the typical lack of provisions of a Rogers' expedition, Van Horne, a portly man, shed many pounds. As they approached a camp in Rogers Pass, Van Horne got a whiff of dinner. It was there, he later reported: "That I learned that a man can smell a ham from ten miles away."

Despite Rogers' flaws, James Hill of the CPR executive

liked him. Rogers had championed a feasible line at a time when one was sorely needed, and when everyone else in the surveying corps doubted that one could be found. Rogers framed the $5000 dollar cheque, finally cashing it at the CPR's request so that the company could balance its books. Hill was so grateful to Rogers, he hired him to survey the mountain section of his Great Northern Railroad. While engaged there in 1887, Rogers' horse pitched him to the ground. The surveyor never recovered from the injuries and died two years later, a few weeks shy of his sixtieth birthday. Another Rogers Pass on the Montana-Idaho border commemorates him.

The Sleepless Knight

The two principals that James Hill hired after Rogers — Alpheus Stickney, General Superintendent, and Thomas Lafayette Rosser, Chief Engineer– did not pan out. Although both were experienced with U.S. railroads, they were out of their league on the CPR project. Hill soon discovered that, by embroiling themselves in land speculations along the proposed route, the pair had netted themselves $130,000 and had compromised the line location. The CPR executive would not tolerate such conflict of interest. Hill convinced Stickney to "resign" in October 1881.

As Stickney's replacement, Hill suggested 38-year-old William Cornelius Van Horne. Van Horne was, and remains, the classic American business success story. Born in rural Illinois in 1843, he was expelled from school at age 14, never to go back. Early in his career, he worked for a telegraph company, where he became so proficient at deciphering the dots and dashes of telegraphy, he could decode a message by ear.

Van Horne's first railway posting was with the Illinois Central Railroad. For the next decade, he hopped from job to job, from platform to platform, from railroad to railroad — whistle stops along a meteoric career path. Legends gathered in his wake. In 1870, Van Horne — not knowing whom he was addressing — reprimanded outlaw Jesse James and his gang, threatening to throw them off a train for harassing a passenger and her child.

Van Horne mastered every detail of railway operations by working holidays, nights, and Sundays. He designed stations and yards. He became a divisional superintendent, and then, at age 28, the youngest railway superintendent in the world. He resurrected a string of railroads and absorbed their competitors. Van Horne's frequent dealings in Minnesota brought him into contact with James Hill, who recommended that the CPR hire the wunderkind as its General Manager.

Van Horne's scope of responsibility was broader than Stickney's had been. It included overseeing sections of railway in eastern Canada that the CPR had taken over from the government. Consequently, the CPR agreed to pay Van Horne $15,000 a year, a salary so outlandish that the company fudged its books to conceal two-thirds of the wage as "construction costs." Given that the final cost of the railway

— including government subsidies and forgiven loans — was $120.5 million, the wage that the CPR paid Van Horne during the next five years was the best money spent on the project.

Van Horne's first act was to pilfer John Egan from the Chicago, Milwaukee and St. Paul Railroad. With his new Superintendent in tow, the General Manager descended on Winnipeg on December 31, 1881. A month later, after he had assessed the work of Chief Engineer Rosser, Van Horne fired him, demanding that he clear his office that afternoon. Not one to do things by halves, Van Horne also dismissed all of Rosser's staff.

Although James Hill had touted Van Horne as "the ablest railway general in the world," many of Van Horne's underlings resented his ways, calling him "the General Boss of Everybody and Everything." People watched their backs and minded their gossip. Van Horne could interpret the clatter of a telegraph transmission while also carrying on a conversation. In railroading, this made him psychic. He was among the earlier multi-taskers. He would appear unannounced at any time, anywhere and everywhere along the line. He would be waiting at drafting tables with a hundred questions when the engineers came to work in their Winnipeg office. A few days, later he might be dealing cards and downing bourbon long into the night in a dormitory car at the end-of-steel.

When he had hired Van Horne, James Hill hoped that his new General Manager would share an opinion. Hill considered the Lake Superior section to be a financial, engineering, and operational nightmare. But the segment had to be completed before the CPR would receive all of its land grant. Hill wanted the Canadian government to allow that part of the railway to be routed along existing lines in the U.S., doing away with the construction headaches while giving the CPR immediate access to the land grant. It was no coincidence that under such a scheme, Hill's Great Northern Railroad would have become part of the CPR route.

But Van Horne answered to no one. Before joining the CPR, he had inspected the route north of Lake Superior and in eastern Manitoba. Although he thought that the Canadian Shield posed "200 miles of engineering impossibilities," he refused to back Hill's argument. Van Horne was already intoxicated by the prospects of fame and power that would accompany fulfillment of the CPR contract. Mere granite and muskeg were no obstacles. When Hill learned of Van Horne's lack of allegiance, he vowed revenge even if he had "to go to hell for it and shovel coal." Van Horne replied: "Well if he does, I'll tear the guts out of his [rail]road."

Van Horne compelled CPR President George Stephen to side with him. Hill quit the CPR to focus on completing the Great Northern Railroad. Curiously, when building his U.S. railway, Hill hired Canadians to positions of importance.

Van Horne became a vice-president of the CPR in May 1884. He was the railroad's greatest champion when it twice teetered on the threshold of ruin. In 1884, when construction costs were topping $1.5 million a month, the government doled out a $22.5-million loan. The funds were spent within a year, chiefly to repay other loans. In 1885, John A. Macdonald, weary beyond all measure, was reluctant to put before Parliament another bill to advance funds to the CPR. He feared that his government would be defeated on the motion, and that the Liberals, once back in power, would not complete the railway.

It took Macdonald months to see the other half of the predicament — without an infusion of cash, the CPR could not complete the project. Using personal funds that amounted to millions of dollars, George Stephen and fellow executive member, Donald Smith, were carrying the railway's day-to-day expenses. Stephen wrote to Macdonald: "... what Smith and I have done and are doing individually, is simply absurd on any kind of business grounds... we are a couple of fools for our pains."

By April 1885, construction crews had been without pay for five months. Van Horne was squashing wildcat strikes all the way from northern Ontario to BC's Selkirk Mountains. Members of Macdonald's cabinet, principally Charles Tupper, pressed Macdonald. To illustrate how indispensable the railway had become, Tupper pointed to the second Northwest (Riel) Rebellion, which had begun in March 1885. Using a plan devised by John Egan and Van Horne, the Canadian government had been able to move 3000 troops to Manitoba in just seven days along the nearly-completed CPR route. Had there been no railway, a government response might have taken three months, as it had during the first Riel Rebellion in 1869. Although the second rebellion was not yet over, it would be quelled. The CPR had already helped to save the country.

The argument raised Macdonald from his stupor. On May 1, 1885, the Prime Minister introduced a new CPR relief bill. It provided for a $35-million issue of bonds to finance completion of the venture, and postponed the repayment by the CPR of $29 million in prior government loans. The government also handed out $500,000 to meet immediate payroll. It took more than two months for the bill to move through Parliament. In the interim, Van Horne's men completed their impossible task along the north shore of Lake Superior, driving the last spike to link Montreal and Winnipeg. Superintendent Egan was pleased: "As to the character of the work, it will remain an everlasting monument to the builders."

On July 10, the day that creditors were ready to call in their debts and force the CPR into receivership, the relief bill passed. CPR President George Stephen then approached Barings in London to see if the bank would purchase some of the bonds. Barings snapped up $13.1 million worth, enough to make possible the completion of the railway. Van Horne rewarded the bank by renaming a siding in BC for one of the directors — Lord Revelstoke.

Perhaps no other undertaking as colossal as the construction of the CPR ever came so close to ruin when so near completion. On the day that the relief bill passed, only two sections remained to be constructed, comprising less than 180 miles in BC. Ironically, one section included Eagle Pass, the breach through the mountains discovered by Walter Moberly almost 20 years earlier.

For his service to Canada and the Commonwealth, Queen Victoria called Van Horne to knighthood in 1890. He declined with the comment: "I would not like such an honour to come to me merely because of my position as president of the Canadian Pacific Railway Company." (He had become president in 1889.) The Queen offered again in 1891, and again Van Horne turned her down. But Her Highness was determined. In 1894, Queen Victoria made Van Horne an Honorary Knight Commander of the Order of St. Michael and St. George. Van Horne did not become a Canadian citizen until 1914, the year before his death. He remains one of a few Americans to have been knighted.

Chapter 6
One Railroad
Too Many

I n the checkerboard world of the mid-1800s, most atlases depicted the countries of the British Commonwealth in a shade of red. Because John A. Macdonald had insisted that the CPR be constructed entirely on Canadian soil, promoters and detractors alike referred to its "all-red route."

By the end of its first decade of operation, the CPR was raking in an annual profit of $15 million. Those who had predicted the railway's demise fell silent. Across the Atlantic Ocean, the executive of the Grand Trunk Railroad lamented not having built Canada's first transcontinental railway. In the 1850s and again in 1880, the Grand Trunk — which had more miles of track in Canada than any other railroad — had been offered the opportunity. On the first occasion, the

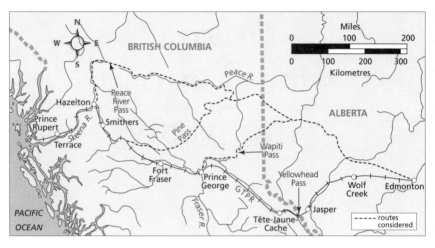

The GTPR in Alberta and BC

Grand Trunk was uninterested and lacked the capital. On the second occasion, it declined to gamble on the all-red route.

In the 1890s, the CPR began cutting into the Grand Trunk's business in eastern Canada. In response, the Grand Trunk cleaned house, appointing Charles Rivers Wilson as its president. Wilson was a career diplomat who had never been to Canada and who knew almost nothing about railways. In 1896, he set out to overhaul the Grand Trunk's operations and to begin transcontinental competition with the CPR. Acknowledging his lack of expertise, Wilson hired, as the Grand Trunk's General Manager, American railway wizard Charles Melville Hays. Wilson hoped that Hays would match the accomplishments of William Cornelius Van Horne.

Hays initially met expectations. He double-tracked

sections of line in eastern Canada, sold track to the CPR, but retained running rights, reduced grades, purchased modern freight cars and passenger cars, and installed air brakes on all rolling stock. Costs went down; profits went up. But whereas Van Horne had made decisions for the CPR with economy foremost in mind, Wilson would soon learn that, after the initial cost-cutting that inevitably follows a spirited change in business command, Hays tended to dream bigger than the bank account.

Hays wanted to expand the Grand Trunk's operations westward, but he soon discovered that the railroad had again waited too long. There was a new kid on the western railway block, the Canadian Northern Railway. Its two opportunistic owners, William Mackenzie and Donald Mann, had bought up flagging railways and unbuilt charters to piece together a ramshackle line centered in — of all places — Manitoba. The Canadian Northern capitalized on the prevailing anti-CPR sentiment among farmers, who were at the mercy of a monopoly. Mackenzie and Mann purchased 3000 bushels of wheat seed and gave it away to settlers, with the result that the Canadian Northern became known as "the farmer's railroad." It would eventually corner 30 percent of the grain market. In 1902, with the completion of "The Muskeg Special" — its line from Winnipeg to Port Arthur — the Canadian Northern operated 1706 miles of track. Its corporate motto was "Energy, Enterprise, Ability." Hays could not help but take notice.

When the Grand Trunk refused to build new track in the west, Hays quit. But the executive lured him back a year later with a commitment to expansion. In response to the Grand Trunk's plans, Mackenzie and Mann sought to complete the Canadian Northern to the Pacific Ocean and to take over the Intercolonial Railway in eastern Canada, making theirs a transcontinental route. But the Intercolonial was not for sale. Mackenzie approached Wilson, proposing that the Grand Trunk would build in the east and the Canadian Northern would build in the west, to create a new transcontinental route on which each railroad would share running rights.

Wilson liked the idea, but Hays would have none of it. During the next two years, Hays played the role of slick Yankee railway baron to the hilt, thinking that it would take little to oust the Canadian railway bumpkins. Hays would have done better to study his rivals and to consider forming a partnership with them.

William Mackenzie, financial mastermind of the Canadian Northern, was a storekeeper and ex-school teacher who had risen to the top of railway contracting by cutting deals and making allies. Donald Mann had abandoned a calling to the ministry to become a blacksmith and then a lumberjack. He handled the technical operations of the Canadian Northern with the gruff manner of a frontiersman. Mann knew how to make enemies and cared little about that reputation. The pair were opposites politically, too; Mackenzie was a Conservative, Mann a Liberal. This unusual alliance won favour in many situations. One of their early deals in Manitoba provided a land grant of five million acres, the sales of which supplied much of their early capital.

Hays first tried to buy out the upstarts, but he balked when Mackenzie and Mann asked $30,000 per mile for their track, and when the Bank of Commerce appraised the company's stock at between $12.5 million and $15 million. Unable to negotiate, Hays began to play dirty. He tried, without success, to convince Prime Minister Wilfred Laurier to withhold the government's guarantee on an issue of Canadian Northern bonds.

He couldn't get rid of Canadian Northern, so Hays decided to out compete it. In 1903, he petitioned the Canadian government to charter the Grand Trunk to build a line from North Bay across the prairies, through Edmonton and along the Skeena River to the Pacific coast. Whereas Mackenzie and Mann were attempting to finance their railway privately, Hays stipulated that the government should take a financial responsibility in his railway's construction. He wanted the government to pay $6400 per mile built and to offer a land grant of 5000 acres per mile.

Prime Minister Wilfred Laurier, a Liberal, received Hays warmly. It was an election year. In the manner that John A. Macdonald had put the Conservative party's stamp on the CPR, Laurier wanted to put a Liberal mark on a competitor that would crack the CPR's monopoly in western Canada. After Laurier had twice failed to broker a deal between Hays and the Canadian Northern, the Prime Minister put forward the idea for the National Transcontinental Railway.

It was a complicated scheme. East of Winnipeg, the Canadian government would lay new steel to stitch together a route, 1844 miles long, to connect with the Intercolonial Railway, whose terminus was at Moncton, New Brunswick. West of Winnipeg, a newly created subsidiary of the Grand Trunk would build a new line, 1752 miles to the Pacific Ocean. This subsidiary, the Grand Trunk Pacific Railroad (GTPR), would rent the eastern section from the government for 30 years with an option to buy. The government would be the major guarantor of the western section, but unlike the earlier deal with the CPR, it refused to issue a land grant. Hays would become the President of the GTPR while maintaining his position with the Grand Trunk.

The CPR was not initially averse to another transcontinental railway. William Cornelius Van Horne commented: "We would hail with delight a parallel route from Atlantic to Pacific to help us develop the country. There is enough of it up there for us all." The prairies were booming. In 1895, settlers had established 2000 homesteads. Within five years another 32,000 homesteads had popped up. The development in 1904 of the Marquis wheat hybrid, which ripened almost two weeks earlier than any other variety, had "rolled back the Arctic a full two hundred miles," permitting crops to be grown much farther north than when the CPR had been built. Fifty thousand American settlers arrived in 1905, the year that Saskatchewan and Alberta entered Confederation.

Although there was strong support in those boom times for a second Canadian transcontinental railway, virtually no one favoured a third. Laurier's plan was characterized as "premature, ill-conceived, immature of design and of dubious national advantage." As the plans of the Canadian Northern and the GTPR unfolded, an underling at the CPR reassessed the situation: "The Canadian Northern has lots of traffic and no railway. The Grand Trunk [Pacific] has a good railway and no traffic. God help us if they ever get together."

After a stormy debate in the House of Commons, Laurier's National Transcontinental bill passed with a margin of six votes in September 1903. Hays sailed to England in February 1904 to meet the GTPR executive. By misrepresenting the degree of financial risk and by touting the potential for trans-Pacific trade, Hays convinced the board of the project's merits. In August 1905, the GTPR turned its first sod at Sand Hill, Manitoba, 110 miles west of Winnipeg. It was not until May 1908 that it began construction eastward from Prince Rupert, which — being 500 nautical miles closer to Tokyo than is Vancouver — Hays had chosen as the western terminus. Hays proclaimed that Prince Rupert, which boasted the third-deepest natural ocean harbour in the world, would become the "Venice of Canada." The government's work on the National Transcontinental got underway in 1906 after 50 survey teams had explored more than 10,000 miles of potential routes, much of it through the empty country of north-central Quebec.

The government made one thing clear to Hays: The new railway would not operate on grades as steep as those of the CPR. The line would have a maximum grade of four-tenths of one percent (21 feet per mile), as opposed to 2.2 percent (116 feet per mile). Nonetheless, construction of the GTPR commenced long before its route across the Rockies was decided. Surveyors explored 40 variations, but four routes were favoured early on: Peace River Pass, Pine Pass, Wapiti Pass, and Sandford Fleming's old favourite, Yellowhead Pass. For every mile of track built, the GTPR surveyed 65 miles of possibilities in western Alberta and in BC.

The GTPR split its construction work into two parcels: the 920-mile Prairie Division from Winnipeg to Wolf Creek (130 miles west of Edmonton), and the 832-mile Mountain Division from Wolf Creek to Prince Rupert. Plotting the route for the Mountain Division fell to C.C. Van Arsdoll, a soft-spoken Texan hired by Hays and characterized by him as "the foremost railway pathfinder on the North American continent."

In 1906, Van Arsdoll secretly reported to his boss that he had located a line within specifications through Yellowhead Pass. (When the GTPR built the line, it exceeded the maximum grade on a 25-mile section of track.) No other transcontinental railway in North America could claim so gentle an overall grade. It meant that in the Rockies the GTPR's locomotives would have seven times the hauling power than those used by the CPR, while consuming much less fuel. Hays celebrated the route: "No wonder there is general belief that the greater part of the traffic across North America will flow over the steel highway [of the GTPR] between Moncton and the Pacific." For his achievement, Van Arsdoll earned the nickname, Four-Tenths Van.

After 1904, the life of a Canadian railway baron became onerous. In response to the proliferation of railroads, Laurier's government created the Board of Railway Commissioners. The Board had the power to meddle in every aspect of railway planning, construction, and operations. In 1905, the GTPR asked the government, via the Board, to provide blanket approval for all of its potential routes to the Pacific Ocean. The government obliged while hoping that the GTPR would build through the Peace River country, which showed the greatest promise for new settlement and agriculture.

In September 1906, the government became aware that the Canadian Northern was about to file plans to cross the Rockies at Yellowhead Pass and to carry on to the Pacific coast. Because the government had a tremendous stake in the GTPR, it asked Hays to immediately file detailed plans for all of its proposed routes. In this manner, by approving the GTPR's plans first, the government would be allowing it to build a line with the best grades.

Rather than have the GTPR's submission debated and delayed in the House of Commons, Collingwood Schreiber,

Chief Engineer for the Department of Railways and Canals, secured two orders-in-council that gave approval to the GTPR's plans. When the Canadian Northern's plans for Yellowhead Pass later emerged from his in-basket, Schreiber blithely told the competitor that its proposed route was a "crooked line" that conflicted with that of the GTPR. The plans could not be accepted because they were not at the same scale as those of the GTPR and did not show a western terminus. Although the Canadian Northern's lawyers smelled the rat and called foul, Schreiber dismissed the application, dealing a severe blow to the railway's viability.

In July 1909, the GTPR's tracks reached Edmonton from the east. The connection was achieved in part by concessions from its competitor. The Canadian Northern not only shipped the trusses for two critical bridges that the GTPR required east of the city, it also built a spur line to one of the bridge sites to deliver the steel.

The following winter the GTPR's construction crews began to tackle the crossing of the Rockies. They would soon have company. After scrambling for two years, Mackenzie and Mann had secured a charter in BC, permitting a subsidiary of the Canadian Northern that would run across Yellowhead Pass to Vancouver. While the GTPR's work gangs cleared the grade and laid track, the Canadian Northern's surveyors leap-frogged along. D.B. Hanna, the Canadian Northern Superintendent, summed up the mood: "There was no cloud in the sky; everything was beautifully blue; western development was going ahead, immigration was entirely satisfactory, and there was plenty of money."

No one could foresee WWI and the Great Depression, which together would snuff out the candle of prosperity. For the next two years, across more than 150 miles of western Alberta and through the Rockies, rival workers constructed the lines of the GTPR and the Canadian Northern side by side in what would soon prove to be the most futile episode in Canadian railway history.

Chapter 7
Paper, Rocks, and Steel

F or the Canadian Pacific, Grand Trunk Pacific, and Canadian Northern, transforming a location survey from a line on a map into railway track necessitated a parade of technology through the landscape.

First came the axemen and teamsters, who opened a right-of-way 100 feet wide. In the case of the GTPR/National Transcontinental, crews working between 1906 and 1914 cleared 3596 miles of line — 68 square miles of Canadian wilderness. On easy ground on the prairies, the clearing crews included 600 men, 550 horses, 260 scrapers, and ten graders. In the mountains, clearing the difficult terrain required 24 steamshovels and 660 horse teams.

The first of the construction engineers followed, establishing camps and a network of wagon roads. In the Rockies, the GTPR spent as much as $1000 a mile on wagon roads. The crossings of large rivers required the installation of cable ferries, often at a cost of $25,000 each. Along one 90-mile section of its Mountain Division, the GTPR spent $4 million constructing roads, camps, and ferries, and $1 million on 30,000 tons of supplies for the work crews that would soon arrive. The railway shipped some survey provisions upstream on the Fraser River, an enterprise in which 50 men drowned in one season.

The GTPR benefited from a technology not available during construction of the CPR. It connected its camps by telephone, facilitating the provisioning of the work and enabling construction engineers to overcome problems quickly. In most cases, the linemen used trees as telephone poles. Many trees in the forests of Canada still bear the insulators of the original line. When the railway was completed, the GTPR took pride in replacing the temporary telephone lines with new ones, strung on posts that were perfect spars spaced equally from each other and at a consistent distance from the track.

This attention to order and neatness — "the British model" in railway building — set the GTPR apart from the CPR and other North American railroads. Taunting the Canadian Northern, Charles Hays bragged: "Railroads are not now built as the earlier [rail]roads were built, uphill, down dale, on an unballasted road bed of mud." Hays was echoing another critic who, in describing the Canadian Northern, quipped that its track "had a regrettable tendency to jump up and kick the trains from behind."

The CPR and the GTPR had different experiences securing labour. With an advertised wage of $1.50 a day, contractors working for the CPR enticed perhaps 20,000 workers onto the prairies in 1882. In 1884-85, another 15,000 toiled north of Lake Superior. As funds dwindled, the railway attempted to chop wages to $1.00 a day — typical pay for a labourer in Toronto or Montreal — while still clawing back $4.50 per week for board.

Thirty years later when the GTPR was under construction, Manitoba, Saskatchewan, and Alberta were already settled and were known collectively as "Canada's one thousand mile farm." Competition with farms for labourers was so intense, the GTPR attracted fewer workers in summer than in winter.

At the peak of construction the GTPR reported that its contractors employed 50,000 across the country. But one worker in the west said that every man counted as being employed included the one who was just quitting and the one being hired to replace him. Many deserted after eyeing the terrain, preferring the possibilities of prospecting to those of railway construction.

When the GTPR began building toward the Rockies in 1910, wages for basic work ranged from $1.70 to $2.00 for a ten-hour day. As construction entered the mountains, workers demanded more money. Strikes were common, especially when crews on the western part of the Mountain Division discovered that those to the east were making more money for the same work. The GTPR attempted to import Chinese labourers to cut costs, but abandoned the idea because of anti-Chinese sentiment in BC. The railway turned to Europe, where it hired 5000 from Scotland and Scandinavia.

In clearing the grades for the CPR and the GTPR, con-tractors were paid according to the type of ground. "Common ground" was loose soil interspersed with rocks of less than one cubic yard in size that could be removed by hand tools. To clear it, the GTPR paid 24 cents per cubic yard. The clearing of "loose rock" — anything harder than common ground but softer than bedrock — required horse teams and was paid at 50-58 cents per cubic yard. "Solid rock" required blasting and often paid more than $30 per linear foot of grade. The loca-tion surveys for the railways provided estimates of how much of each type of ground would be encountered. Contractors based their fortunes on those estimates.

Where clearing work was not assigned by contract, the GTPR used the "station man" system. The company paid $40 per acre to station men — so named because each was stationed at a particular point on the line. An acre amounted to about 400 feet of right-of-way. Working alone on common ground, a crack station man could make ten dollars a day — a fortune in 1910.

The rails laid on the GTPR were made of steel, not iron, and weighed 85 lbs. per yard. (Modern rails weigh 132 lbs. per yard.) Each mile of track and attendant sidings consumed 3000 ties, typically hewn from surrounding forests. In all on the GTPR, 13,700,000 ties were used, upon which navvies spiked 540,000 tons of rails. Originally budgeted at $60,000 per mile with a completion date of 1911, the cost of the GTPR's Mountain Division — which included 26 bridges built of concrete and steel — was $93,307,184, or $112,000 per mile. The final cost of the entire railway, completed in 1914, was $140 million. As the GTPR's completion date approached and passed unfulfilled, detractors began to refer to the railroad as the Grand Trafficker of Promises Railway.

One episode from the construction of the GTPR demonstrated the magnitude of the problems confronted by construction crews, and the ingenuity with which they created solutions. About 28 miles west of the MacLeod River (between Edmonton and Jasper, Alberta) the location survey indicated that the crest of a hill should be removed. The construction engineer estimated that the work would require steamshovels, a locomotive, and dump cars. But if the grading crew had waited for the rails to be completed from the east to deliver the equipment, track-laying would have been delayed for weeks as crews levelled the offending hummock and trucked away the spoil.

Frederick Talbot, who wrote a book about the construction of the GTPR, walked the right-of-way west from

Edmonton in 1911. Far beyond the end-of-steel, he came across a work train on a haphazard set of rails, taking down the crest of a hill. "I was somewhat puzzled [about how the train had traversed the prairie]," he wrote, "until, seated round the blazing camp fire at night, the [grading] engineer volunteered an explanation." An excavation train had been specially dispatched to the end-of-steel, where work gangs had dismantled the 60-ton locomotive, two steamshovels, and a set of dump cars. After labelling each part, the men packed the myriad pieces onto makeshift sleds. Hundreds of mules and horses skidded the sleds the 28 miles to the base of the problem hill. There the workers reassembled the hardware and set it upon temporary rails. The tactic worked. By the time the end-of-steel arrived, the problem hill was no more. Track-laying proceeded west without delay.

The GTPR line in western Alberta was notorious for "slipping ground" or "blue clay" — banks of saturated soil on or just under the grade. Slipping ground usually became evident after the track was finished, when the motion and weight of trains would cause the soil to liquefy. The track would slither sidehill or downhill, necessitating a closure of the line and costly reconstruction.

In northwestern Ontario, the CPR and the GTPR encountered what workers, with remarkable composure, simply called "bad places." Joseph Whitehead's experience on the 37 miles of Contract 15 on the CPR at the Ontario-Manitoba border, exemplified the problems. Whitehead had won the $500,000 contract in 1877 after a protracted and corrupt bidding process. He expected a $200,000 profit on the short segment.

When Whitehead's men began work, rails were being laid west from Lake Superior and east from Manitoba. Contract 15 was in the centre of the 400-mile gap, so his crews had to haul in every piece of equipment — including small work trains and the first steamshovel to work on the CPR.

But the logistical problems of getting to Contract 15 were trifling compared to the work itself. The open, flat areas of the Canadian Shield concealed two features that were the bane of railways — sinkholes and muskegs. The sinkholes were areas of permafrost that appeared to be solid in winter, but that turned into quivering masses of goo as the weather warmed. A sinkhole would often support the weight of foot traffic and equipment traffic as the right-of-way was cleared, but as the grade was completed, tracks were laid, and work trains advanced, it might collapse, swallowing locomotives and equipment in seconds. Muskegs — the prolific, scrub-covered peat swamps of the Shield country — although more obvious to the eye, were a greater problem. A later traveller described them as "porridge sewn with razorblades." The remedy for sinkholes and muskegs was the same: attempt to fill them.

Every load dropped into the gummy depths took a chunk out of profits. Worse, crews soon learned that success was never guaranteed. Many a causeway disappeared overnight. Some collapsed after being left to settle for days. The depths of these failures could be mind-boggling; some exceeded 50 feet. The track across one sinkhole collapsed seven times, claiming three locomotives and miles of steel. Engineers attempted all manner of fixes, including draining the muskegs or driving pilings on which to dump the fill. But in most cases, the pilings either never reached solid bottom or hit bedrock so far down as to be impracticable.

At six miles across, the Julius Muskeg in northwestern Ontario was the largest on the CPR. At least three other muskegs (one of them on Contract 15) each consumed more than 200,000 cubic yards of fill without yielding a solid grade. In one case, crews excavated an adjacent hill in its entirety, dumped it load by load into a muskeg, and still could not find the bottom. Thirty-five years later, when the Canadian Northern built through muskeg country, one 15-mile stretch required 2.6 miles of trestles. To counter muskeg on the isthmus at Rainy Lake, the railway built what was at the time the longest causeway in North America.

As resources were exhausted and seasons slipped by, construction engineers resorted to advancing the lines across the worst places atop floating latticeworks of timber. These muskeg mattresses each consumed tens of thousands of spindly pine and black spruce. They subsequently posed a nightmare for locomotive crews, as the rail bed would undulate beneath trains. Long after the CPR officially opened, crews continued to pour fill into the bad places until they became stable causeways. The GTPR learned from its rival's earlier experiences; it usually sank a muskeg mattress by piling the railway grade atop it, creating a permanent railbed more quickly.

It is not surprising that many contractors working for the CPR failed. Although the government had paid extra charges that nearly doubled what he had bid, Joseph Whitehead went bankrupt on Contract 15 in just over a year. Throwing good money after bad, the government had no choice but to assume the work. It took seven years to complete the 467 miles between Lake Superior and Manitoba.

Muskegs were the horrors of the open country, but routine cutting and filling along sections of hilly grade often demanded the movement of astounding quantities of material. On the GTPR line at Brulé Lake, just east of Jasper, one cut involved 87,000 cubic yards. A nearby embankment consumed 117,000 cubic yards of fill.

Construction engineers sometimes used desperate tactics. Along the north shore of Lake Superior, preparations for track-laying on the CPR continued during the winter of 1883-84. Crews placed the rails atop the snow, attempting to follow the surveyed line which was sometimes 20-30 feet beneath the drifts. The engineers had hoped to speed up track-laying in the spring, but when the rails melted out, the steel often came to rest far from the intended right-of-way.

The granite hummocks of the Canadian Shield, dotted with thousands of lakes, alternately dictated a sinuous line or the need for blasting. The CPR was the first railway to make prolific use of nitroglycerine. It is difficult to say which was more wild, the landscape or the explosive. Nitro is a pale yellow, toxic oil that is extremely unstable. It is liquid at temperatures above +11° C. When solid the substance is still dangerous, but it can be transported much more safely. William Cornelius Van Horne built three nitroglycerine plants along the north shore of Lake Superior to minimize the distances that his contractors would have to ship the explosive. Each plant produced 2000 lbs. daily. As most of the blasting on the CPR was carried out in summer, the workers usually dealt with nitro in its liquid form, and with predictable results. Liquid nitro could not be packed in carts where it might have exploded at the first bump. Men carried it on their backs in ten-gallon tins that often leaked onto the rocks. The dribbles would then explode underfoot, dismembering or killing the next man, mule or horse to pass by.

To create a blasting hole, workers known as rock-hogs bored with hand tools or air-powered drills. They poured water into the hole to tamp the charge and then added the nitro, which, being heavier, sank to the bottom. Joseph Whitehead's company spent more than $300,000 on nitroglycerine on Contract 15. Another section on the CPR, 90 miles long, consumed $10 million worth of nitro. When Sandford Fleming travelled the route of the CPR in 1883, he counted 30 graves in 50 miles in northwestern Ontario. All of the dead had been killed in blasting accidents.

When the GTPR tackled the Shield country to the north of the CPR's route, its rock-hogs used dynamite — a more stable explosive that contains 75 percent nitro. One of the rock cuts in eastern Manitoba required six months to prepare. Five thousand dollars worth of dynamite was detonated in a single explosion that moved 14,000 cubic yards of rock, estimated to weigh 30,000 tons.

The GTPR expended tremendous sums blasting its Prince Rupert yards from the oceanfront, and in making the railbed along the Skeena and Bulkley rivers. In its first 212 miles east from Prince Rupert, the GTPR required 13 tunnels. Between Prince Rupert and the Kitselas Canyon — a distance of about 100 miles — crews moved four million cubic yards of rock. Some of the cuts were 60 feet deep; one was 6600 feet long, requiring two years to prepare. On this section, rock-hogs set more than two million blasts, using ten million lbs. of explosives, with a value of $1 million.

At the Kitselas Canyon, the end-of-steel was held up for a year as rock-hogs blasted four tunnels, totalling 6000 feet. To save time, the rock-hogs would hang in harnesses, swinging out of the way before the charges detonated. One morning the lead rock-hog at the smaller Kitselas tunnel miscounted the number of explosions by one. Eight men swung back into place too soon. The blasting crew hurriedly summoned a doctor, but little of the men remained.

Chapter 8
Railhead, Roadhouse, and Ruin

The Canadian Pacific, Grand Trunk Pacific, and Canadian Northern were pioneering railroads, built for the most part across lands unsettled by white people and with no means of supply other than their own rails. With its connection — via the Pembina Branch line — to the St. Paul, Minneapolis and Manitoba Railway in the U.S. Midwest, Winnipeg was admirably placed to become the railhead for the CPR as it built across the prairies.

When the CPR set up shop in Winnipeg early in 1882, the community boomed. Although promoters dubbed it the "Chicago of the North," construction worker Morley Roberts was less charitable, describing it as "an entirely execrable, flourishing and detestable business town, flat ugly and new. The climate is said to be two months black flies, two months dust, and the remainder of the year mud and snow." In its sprawling Winnipeg yards, the CPR amassed rails, bridge materials, rocks, gravel, ties, coal, cordwood, food, animal feed, and a myriad other materials for the push west. The CPR would require so much steel, Canadian and U.S. mills could not produce enough; most was imported from England and Germany. Contractors and subcontractors invaded the town. Labourers arrived by the thousands, signing on for the free trip west, the passage to be docked from their pay.

Eleven years after its surveyors had taken to the field, the Canadian government had built only 143 miles of the transcontinental railway. Although the CPR absorbed 254 miles of an Ontario railway in 1881, the company itself laid only 131 miles of new track that year. In response, the CPR's new superintendent, John Egan, outsourced the construction work, awarding a colossal contract to the firm of Langdon and Shepard of Minneapolis-St. Paul. The critics again cried foul; more Americans were stealing Canadian thunder. But it had been three decades since Canada had built a trunk railway line; the country simply lacked the expertise. In accepting the work, Langdon and Shepard agreed to fulfill William Cornelius Van Horne's outrageous promise to build 500 miles of track in 1882.

Henry Ford or Ransom E. Olds are often credited with creating the world's first industrial assembly line, but the recognition might go to John Egan and the company of Langdon and Shepard for the manner in which they organized work on the Canadian prairies. The company hired 300 subcontractors, eventually employing 7600 men and 1700 horse teams. In the next 16 months, while making the grade to Calgary, crews moved ten million cubic yards of prairie soil and scrub, installed more than 1,500,000 ties and 150,000 tons of rails, and used 3.65 million board feet of lumber in bridges, trestles, and pilings.

In 1881, the CPR had averaged less than a mile of new track a day. By July 1882, the crews of Langdon and Shepard, working six, ten-hour days a week, were making two miles a day. With Van Horne constantly in their faces threatening to cancel subcontracts, workers raised this to 3.2 miles a day by the end of August, and on two days that month laid just over four miles of track. Work proceeded so quickly, surveyor J.H. Secretan complained that grading crews were passing him at night, clearing terrain that had not been staked for the final location.

By autumn the supply system collapsed. Sometimes the tracklayers would sit idle for days after reaching a bridge site for which the timbers had not been delivered. Sometimes supply trains would derail while running over newly completed track. At the onset of winter, locomotive crews, seeking water for the boilers, could not find sources that were not frozen. The productivity declined to 2.6 miles per day in September and to one mile per day by December.

To compensate, Langdon and Shepard moved to a seven-day workweek, taking no rest at Christmas.

When work stopped in early January 1883, the CPR boasted 418 miles of new mainline, 110 miles of branch line, and 57 miles of sidings. In appreciation, the CPR awarded Langdon and Shepard the contract to complete the next 200 miles to Calgary. But before that work could begin in 1883, much of the track had to be extricated from a morass of mud and then rebuilt. The freezing and thawing of winter and spring, coupled with the tremendous construction traffic, had caused many slumps on the grade. Later in the summer of 1883, crews encountered another consequence of winter track-laying. They had left insufficient room for the rails to expand in the heat. This caused buckling and kinking which, in two cases, threw the track completely off the grade.

With greater refinements to their system, the crews of Langdon and Shepard sped across Saskatchewan and Alberta in June 1883, averaging 3.46 miles per day. On July 3, they laid 4.68 miles of track near Regina. Four days later, 6.02 miles were set and spiked. On July 28, near Strathmore, Alberta, they set a single day Canadian record for track-laying — 6.38 miles — including 500 feet that was set and spiked in less than five minutes. On that day, the crews used 16,000 ties and 2200 sections of rail. Navvies set 63,000 spikes, each of which required an average of four blows. The effort was not solely the result of inspired labour. Langdon and Shepard had staged the show, hoping to beat the Union Pacific's

1869 record of ten miles of new track in a day. Although they fell short, the effort contributed greatly to the CPR's cause. Langdon and Shepard completed their contract to Calgary on time in mid-August. Van Horne was so impressed, he named the last two sidings for the partners.

End-of-Steel

Track-laying on the prairies revolved around an ephemeral, artificial community known as end-of-steel. It was the tip of a colossal logistical pyramid whose bulwarks reached back along recently constructed track to intervening depots and the marshalling yards at Winnipeg. Strung out along the way was a huge support staff that included everything from shoemakers to vets. End-of-steel incorporated enough dormitory and dining cars to sleep and feed 300 workers, and administrative cars for CPR officials and contractors.

End-of-steel advanced in half-mile increments. Each step was provisioned by a supply train of 30 cars, packed with 1100 tons of carefully inventoried ties, rails, fishplate connectors, and spikes. As the train was broken apart, small mountains of railway ties appeared at trackside. Drovers brought forward mule teams and carts to pick up the ties, 30 to a cart. As the carts moved along, workers lobbed the ties onto the grade, where two men positioned them, each two-feet away from the previous. Because the ties might be of unequal lengths, the workers aligned the right-hand ends (looking ahead) to be flush.

The rails came next, on flat cars hauled by horse teams along either side of the grade. Normally, six workers would lift a 30-foot, 560 lb. rail from a cart, putting the steel roughly into place on the ties. But legendary Big Jack could pick up a rail without help. Two men measured the spacing at the western ends of the rails, aligning them to standard gauge — four-feet, eight and one-half inches. Four workers attached the new rails to the previous rails, bolting them together with iron connectors called fishplates. Using pry bars, four other men counter-levered under the ties at the fishplates as navvies drove home the spikes that secured the rails.

The navvies' rhythmic hammering as they hopped from tie to tie earned them the nickname, gandy dancers. The most commonly cited origin of the epithet is a railroad myth: most of the tools used in track-laying in the late 1800s — mauls, jacks, and prybars — were supposedly made by the Gandy Manufacturing Company of Chicago. No such company ever existed. A more likely source of the nickname was that as a navvy swung the maul, his head bobbed up and down like a gander's.

After the rails were set, the railbed was ready for ballast. Workers jacked up the track as dump carts delivered crushed rock over it. The ballast helped to level the track, provided drainage, and added a small measure of cushioning, permitting the rails to shift slightly under the weight of trains. In its haste to get the track open, the CPR often skimped on ballasting or omitted it altogether. This resulted in an uneven track and in delays for reconstruction.

When it laid track, the GTPR benefited from technology that had not been available to the CPR 30 years earlier. The Pioneer Track Layer, nicknamed the "praying mantis" or "the gibbet" because of similarities to both, allowed crews to lay 2-3 miles of track in a 15-hour day. The Pioneer was a flat car with two steam engines and a superstructure with a derrick attached. Ties and rails were fed forward along a series of rollers on each side of the car. The ties dropped into place from a trough at the front. Workers walking in advance of the Pioneer aligned and spaced the ties. The derrick operator would then pluck two rails from the car and lower them onto the ties. The crews would bolt the new rails to the preceding rails, spiking them to only every third tie so that the Pioneer could advance quickly. To the rear of the Pioneer, work trains shunted flat cars to and from end-of-steel, while another gang completed the alignment and spiking. The Pioneer could lay a mile of track without resupply. Thirty men worked the forward end of the machine. The CPR had required five times that many to accomplish the same tasks.

The telegraph crews followed the track-layers. On the CPR they installed 1600 miles of line in 1882, ensuring that the foremen at end-of-steel were never out of touch with their supply masters in Winnipeg or with the intervening depots. When the track-laying was completed, fencers enclosed the right-of-way to keep livestock off the track.

The CPR fencing, more than the railbed itself, became a metaphor for the end of the traditional way of life for the Blackfoot (Nitsitapi) First Peoples. Blackfoot hunters had criss-crossed the prairies for thousands of years in pursuit of bison. By the 1880s — as a result of wanton killing of bison by whites and by First Peoples — the bison were gone. The Blackfoot Chief, Crowfoot (Sapomaxicow), had seen the changes coming and knew the futility of resisting: in 1877, he signed Treaty Seven, placing his people on reservations.

When the CPR end-of-steel reached the outskirts of the Blackfoot reserve at Gleichen, east of Calgary, in July 1883, the Blackfoot — fearing that they were about to lose some of their reserve — became militant. Crowfoot dispatched messengers to tell the work gangs to cease, but they refused. Seven hundred warriors would have attacked if not for the intervention of Father Lacombe, an Oblate missionary. Lacombe cabled Van Horne, who directed that all work should stop until the priest could mediate a resolution. Lacombe and Crowfoot were old friends. The chief took the priest's advice to back down. The government later added land to the reserve to compensate for the CPR right-of-way.

As end-of-steel headed over the western horizon, the CPR's carpenters constructed stations, section houses, and water tanks. Painters added the finishing touches and erected signs. Before their work was dry, another section of railway was open for business. The first settlers were often on the next train, riding on flat cars or in boxcars with their few possessions

The Railroad Frontier

End-of-steel rarely remained anywhere long enough for an attendant community to develop. But in two cases on the CPR, at Laggan (now Lake Louise) and Beavermouth, short-lived settlements flourished in a truly western way as the pace of track-laying slowed in the mountains. The community that developed at Laggan late in 1883 became known as "Summit City" for its proximity to the crossing of the Rockies. That winter, 500 men stayed to cut 20,000 cords of wood and 500,000 railway ties for the following season. Mainstreet was a stump-filled clearing, onto which fronted an assortment of tents and rough cabins that bore signs proclaiming themselves as hotels, billiard halls, laundries, and diners. Generally, if a "hotel" was two-storeys tall, it offered legitimate accommodation; otherwise, it was a front for peddling liquor. "Summit City" prospered during 1884 as the supply depot for crews working across Kicking Horse Pass. A year later, the siding remained but the "city" was gone.

Beavermouth was cloistered at the confluence of the Beaver River and the Columbia River, on the eastern approach to Rogers Pass. The community of 2500 — which, among other things, boasted 40 saloons — achieved notoriety in the spring of 1885 after the CPR pay car failed to appear for three months. It says a great deal about the nature of employer-employee relationships of the day that the men, after toiling a winter in the mountains without pay, were still on the job. As spring arrived, many needed money, not necessarily for their own spending — although acquiring liquor was a principal expense — but to send to their homesteads or relatives.

In a letter to Van Horne, James Ross, superintendent of the Mountain Division, characterized the contingent at Beavermouth: "We have some of the worst cut throats on this work that I ever met. They are the refuse and refugees of the western States and Canada... They are prepared to make trouble whenever they get a chance." That trouble was not long in coming. On March 21, 1885, Ross sent Van Horne a coded telegraph:

WORK SUFFERING FOR MONEY. MEN DISSATISFIED AND NOT WORKING PROPERLY. HAVE HAD SEVERAL SMALL STRIKES. CAN YOU SEND BALANCE TRANSFER MONDAY.

When the money arrived, it paid wages for only January and February. In desperation, Ross cashed his own cheques to put towards the payroll. Early in April, he turned for help to Inspector Sam Steele of the North West Mounted Police. Steele, a Mountie since 1873, had been assigned to police the CPR's construction across the prairies and into the mountains. Throughout his career, Steele consistently demonstrated a kind of policing prescience, always being where he was needed. Although he was at Beavermouth as the pot of trouble boiled over, an attack of tick-borne fever consigned him to bed. Unable to even raise his head, he prepped his eight constables and deputized Ross and his colleagues.

Many of the labourers stopped work and began to walk the grade to end-of-steel to incite others to do the same. On the way, they sabotaged bridgework, bringing construction to a halt. Although 300 armed strikers patrolled the line, James Ross went to end-of-steel to reopen the bridge and keep the track-layers on the job. When approached by a mob, Ross took command of a locomotive and steamed to safety as the insurgents opened fire.

The climax came when one of the Mounties arrested a drunk. An angry crowd mobbed the officer and freed the prisoner. Steele, still bed-ridden, sent his deputy and two constables to arrest the man again. This time, 200 strikers surrounded the Mounties, who retreated to seek their boss's instruction. The order was simple: "... shoot anyone who interferes with the arrest!"

The three Mounties got their man on the next attempt, but as they dragged him away 700 strikers followed, brandishing weapons. Steele, who had crawled to the window of his barracks to view the scene, seized a rifle and staggered to the bridge over the Beaver River. As his subordinates gathered behind him, Steele asked the local magistrate to read the Riot Act. The Mountie trained his weapon on the crowd, threatening to mow down any who did not disperse. The warning subdued the throng. Although the strikers stayed off the job until they were paid, there was no more serious trouble.

The Grand Trunk Pacific and Canadian Northern also spawned bawdy communities at end-of-steel. Construction crews for both railways occupied "Mile 29," west of Yellowhead Pass between 1910 and 1914. Little record remains of Mile 29 or the siding called Resplendent that replaced it, except a newspaper comment written during the construction era: "Mile 29 had a reputation of which its inhabitants refused to be proud." There is a graveyard at Resplendent, in which 60 victims of the 1918 flu epidemic are interred.

The greatest story of a boom and bust community on the railways of the west is that of Tete Jaune Cache, BC. In 1907, Tete Jaune Cache consisted of a few prospectors' cabins and the tepees of a band of the Shuswap (Secwepemc) First Peoples. Sounding like a huckster's sales pitch, a government report proclaimed that the settlement would become "the future Spokane of the north." At the height of railway construction in 1912, it was home to 2000 people, making it the largest community in BC north of Kamloops.

The reality of Tete Jaune Cache, as described by Anglican missionary J. Burgon Bickersteth, was anything but glamorous: "It is the usual medley of shacks and tents, pool rooms and stores, a barber's shop, and all the other accompaniments, good and bad, of such a community." The one thing common to people of all circumstances at Tete Jaune Cache was mud. Ankle deep, knee deep, thigh deep — mud was the glue of the GTPR grade from Edmonton to Fort George (now Prince George).

In 1912, the construction firm of Foley, Welch and Stewart initiated sternwheeler service on the upper Fraser River at Tete Jaune Cache. While building the GTPR east from Prince Rupert, the contractors had used two steamboats — *The Conveyor* and *The Operator*. With work there complete, the boats steamed to Victoria. Crews dismantled the vessels and loaded their 25-ton engines and ironworks onto ten freight cars. The parts were shipped on the CPR to Calgary, then to Edmonton, and then back west along the GTPR to rail's end at Red Pass Junction. Workers skidded the hardware the remaining 25 miles to Tete Jaune Cache. One man was killed on the last leg of the journey.

Lumberjacks felled logs at Moose Lake and floated them down the Fraser River to a "shipyard" at Tete Jaune Cache, where the wood was sawn to rebuild the vessels. In this roundabout fashion, *The Conveyor* and *The Operator* were restored to service, to make the 180-mile journey down river to Fort George.

They were big boats — 155 feet long and 36 feet wide — each capable of carrying 200 passengers and a 300-ton cargo. But the vessels had too much draught for the shallows of the upper Fraser River. With their schedule reduced to periods of high water, they offered unreliable service. In 1914, the end-of-steel moved west of Fort George, concluding the brief promise of nautical commerce.

Poised as it was on the doorstep of greatness, Tete Jaune Cache failed to make the transition to transportation centre. Soon after the GTPR commenced operation, WWI began, disrupting the mainly British financing of the railway. Nature also had a hand in the collapse. Floods on the Fraser River inundated the town. After WWI, Tete Jaune Cache became just another railway siding. None of its original buildings survives.

Besides being the hub of the CPR's prairie operations, Winnipeg was the centre for the attendant real estate boom of the 1880s. The government allotted the CPR's 25-million acre land grant in mile-wide blocks on alternating sides of the line west from Winnipeg. Each block in this Railway Belt was 20 miles deep. Homesteaders who settled on the non-CPR lands in the Railway Belt claimed sections of 640 acres (one square mile). They could win title to their land by paying ten dollars and by living on it for three years. Many homesteaders were impostors — speculators and scam artists who crowded the railway line in the hope of grabbing a piece of land that would be within the limits of a new railway boomtown. They would hastily erect a tent and run a quick furrow before heading back to Winnipeg to sell their "developed lot" through unscrupulous land companies. Many an unwary settler was thus duped into buying a lot that was nothing more than two cart tracks in the mud, perhaps within earshot of the railway.

Several factors dictated the placement of railway stations along the CPR and the GTPR. Steam locomotives were powered by cordwood in the 1880s, by coal in the 1890s, and by oil after the 1910s. Whatever the fuel, the tenders required replenishing about every 125 miles. This was also the preferred distance for passenger travel during an 8-hour day, and for a freight train crew to travel in a 10-hour shift. So the railways established divisional points — complete with service yards, roundhouses, and crew quarters — every 125 miles on the prairies and at lesser intervals in the mountains. Examples on the CPR were Ignace, Rat Portage (now Kenora), Brandon, Broadview, Moose Jaw, Swift Current, Medicine Hat, Gleichen, Canmore, Field, Donald, Kamloops, and North Bend. Although Calgary and Regina predated the CPR, these communities were at the wrong mile boards, so the railway disregarded them as divisional points.

The main lines of the CPR and the GTPR were single-tracked, necessitating sidings at short intervals to enable trains to pass by each other. These sidings — which, for safety and economic reasons had to be on level grades — each accommodated a telegraph operator and a section house that was home to a maintenance crew. A siding might also provide an emergency water source for locomotives.

The railway planners knew that most settlers would be travelling by horse and cart to meet trains. A round-trip of 20 miles was a long day's journey in the era before the automobile, so the railways situated their sidings at intervals of six to ten miles.

Two matters determined an "instant" railway town's longevity: the local prosperity of farming, mining, and logging; and whether the siding was required as a divisional point or as a base for extra railway operations. Canmore was a CPR siding that exemplified both. Canmore had coal mines nearby and was where the railway added and disengaged the more powerful locomotives used to cross the Rockies. At Laggan, Field, Donald, and Revelstoke, the CPR added pusher locomotives for the Kicking Horse Pass and Rogers Pass grades. So these sidings, with their roundhouses and yards, endured. The sidings of Banff, Laggan, Field, Glacier, Three Valley, Sicamous, and North Bend were bolstered by tourism after the CPR constructed hotels.

But, as the history of Donald siding attests, nothing lasts forever in railroading. When the CPR found that the distance between Donald and Kamloops was too great to be covered by one crew, the company moved its division point west from Donald to Revelstoke. Donald became a pusher station for the Rogers Pass grade. In 1916, the CPR opened the Connaught Tunnel beneath Rogers Pass, spelling the end for Glacier House hotel in the pass, for the small railway community of Rogers Pass, and for the Donald pusher station.

In creating the matrix of settlement in western Canada, the CPR and the GTPR exercised tremendous influence, deciding where communities would be located and what they would be named. As most members of the CPR executive were

Scots, they chose Scottish names for many sidings. Canmore, Banff, Eldon, Laggan, Leanchoil (lee-AN-coil), Clanwilliam, and Craigellachie (creg-AH-lack-ee) are examples.

Squatters and speculators swarmed along the CPR right-of-way like flies on dung, plunking down in makeshift cabins and tents, awaiting the arrival of end-of-steel and an anticipated offer from the railway to buy them out. What happened at Calgary typified the CPR's response.

The original settlement of Fort Calgary, which dated from the fur trade, occupied the east bank of the Elbow River just above its confluence with the Bow River. The land on the west bank of the Elbow River was a government lot, used to pasture the horses of the North West Mounted Police. Because the settlement existed prior to the railway, it seemed, to squatters who took up residence in 1883, that Fort Calgary would endure.

In June 1883, the CPR's grading crews moved through Fort Calgary, followed by a crew that built a bridge across the Elbow River. The tracks were laid on August 12. Three days later a train pulling an empty boxcar arrived. To the collective disappointment of the community, the train did not stop but carried on across the Elbow River, where it deposited the boxcar on a hastily built siding in the government pasture. Although Van Horne and the executive of the CPR visited Fort Calgary in late August, none of the officials would say where the railway would establish its town. The CPR left the squatters, speculators, and a few legitimate businesses to freeze half the winter away in uncertainty before lowering the boom on their community.

In January 1884, the government — no doubt at the prompting of the railway — released its hold on the horse pasture. The CPR decreed that the boxcar and siding were the new Calgary station. The government responded by moving the post office from across the Elbow River. Fort Calgary was doomed. The settlers and businesses relocated to lots that they were obliged to purchase from the CPR's land company. Many took their tents and clapboard buildings with them, skidding them across the frozen river. Similar scenarios played out in Brandon, Regina, and Vancouver.

The GTPR's land dealings began in 1906 when the BC government sold 10,000 acres at the site of Prince Rupert to an American businessman who was a friend of the railway's construction contractor. The sale, at $1 per acre, was made without consulting BC voters.

The transaction set the tone for the GTPR's real estate operations. The railway established the Grand Trunk Pacific Development Company, which purchased 45,000 acres in advance of the railway's construction and created more than 120 "paper" towns. The first towns constructed on the prairies were named in an alphabetical sequence from east to west. The GTPR named division points after its board members. When it changed the name of Jasper to Fitzhugh in 1911, the town responded with fury. The GTPR waited until Vice-President Fitzhugh resigned before changing the name back.

To christen its western terminus, the GTPR ran a contest with a $250 prize. Entries were to be no more than three syllables or ten letters long. Nonetheless, the executive selected Prince Rupert, suggested by a Winnipeg school teacher. To keep the peace, it awarded two equal prizes to entrants who had kept to the rules by suggesting Port Rupert.

The GTPR was even more cavalier than the CPR when dealing with those who settled in advance of the rails. For the central of its three divisional points between Prince Rupert and Prince George, the GTPR chose the locality known as Hubert, about 16 miles east of present day Smithers. When it came time to plan the station and accompanying town, the GTPR discovered that a Vancouver land company had purchased the district lots. Rather than deal with the company, the GTPR established its divisional point at a new instant town that it named Smithers after the Grand Trunk President. By all accounts, Smithers was a 5-mile wide swamp, plagued with quicksand. The principal feature of what became the main street was a drainage ditch, bridged with planks that led to the front doors of businesses. The post office was built atop pilings sunk 60 feet deep. Smithers has prospered, but poor drainage plagues the community to the present day.

The situation that unfolded at Hazelton (the most northerly point on the GTPR) exemplified how the railway undermined its own profitability and alienated the people it was to serve. The Hazelton area was already noted for mining when the GTPR announced its route in 1908. Anticipating the rail link, mining companies collectively invested more than $1 million in old claims, new prospecting, and infrastructure.

Rail access to Hazelton was not possible because of a canyon upstream on the Bulkley River. It was clear that a New Hazelton would have to be created with the arrival of the railway. Because the rail line would be sandwiched between mountains and rivers, there was only one favourable site for the new community. The GTPR pledged to build its station there, but again found that it had to purchase the necessary land from others. In this case, those others — aware that they were sitting on choice ground — would not sell one-half interest in the new townsite to the railway. So the GTPR's land commissioner purchased a half share in a district lot three miles to the southwest to create another new settlement, South Hazelton, where the railway determined to build its station.

In contrast to the level grade at New Hazelton, the rail line at South Hazelton was "a corkscrew curve on a maximum grade." The miners were outraged because to ship their ore to South Hazelton would cost four dollars per ton more than if they shipped it to New Hazelton. The miners and the principal land owner in New Hazelton appealed to the Board of Railway Commissioners, winning a ruling that humiliated the GTPR by directing it to build its station at New Hazelton and forbidding it to build one at South Hazelton. The Board chastised the GTPR: "If a private individual had done what this company through its officials have done... he ought to be landed in the Penitentiary."

The GTPR was able to overturn the decision, but with prospects for economic development uncertain, three-quarters of the lot holders at South Hazelton abandoned the community. Rather than acquiesce, the GTPR continued to goad the residents of New Hazelton by delaying the construction of a railway station there and by levying freight charges that all but destroyed the local mining industry.

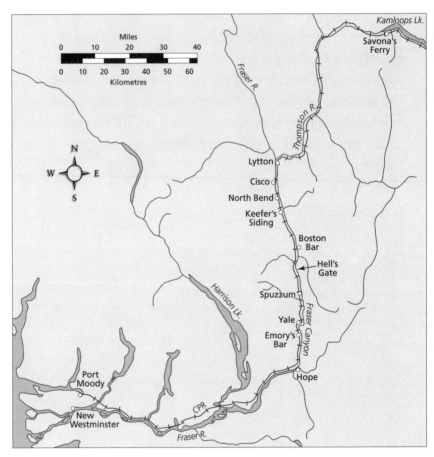

Fraser Canyon 1879–1885

Chapter 9
A Spike as Good as Any Other

W ith William Cornelius Van Horne press-
ing for solutions, the CPR's construction
engineers and contractors scrambled to
piece together gaps on the line in 1882. West of the Selkirk
Mountains in BC, the construction contracts predated Van
Horne. In 1878 and 1879, Sandford Fleming had awarded four
contracts to an American consortium. The work covered 212
miles, with a value of $9,100,000. As its chief contractor, the
consortium selected Andrew Onderdonk. The government's
Chief Engineer, Marcus Smith, kept tabs on Onderdonk, so
Van Horne — who doubtless would have had a suggestion or
three — was obliged to keep his mouth shut.

As his General Manager, Onderdonk hired Michael
Haney, who had worked on sections of the CPR in Manitoba

and Ontario. Haney had a reputation as a wild man who brooked no excuses. Once, when short of supplies, rather than send a memo requesting more, Haney raced to the CPR's yards in Winnipeg where he "borrowed" two carloads of spikes.

In a project brimming with difficulties, Onderdonk grappled with terrain in which the challenges never relented. He was charged with constructing the line through the canyons of the lower Fraser River and the Thompson River, without impinging on the Cariboo Road wagon route.

Simon Fraser, for whom the Fraser River is named, had described its canyon as "one of the worst places in the world." Henry Cambie, Onderdonk's location engineer, sometimes hung from ropes in the canyon as he plotted the line. He went shoeless for the task, believing that bare feet gave better grip on the slick rock. Cambie could find no way out of the canyon or around its mini-headlands, only through. Blasting, tunnelling, and bridging became the hallmarks of the work, with the result that progress was slow, and costs always above estimates. There were 14 tunnels in the 20 miles between Yale and Boston Bar alone; the longest was 1600 feet. One sequence of four tunnels took 18 months to construct.

Onderdonk required a huge labour force. Some estimates claim that he employed 10,000. Two-thirds of his workers were Chinese, many of whom immigrated from the U.S., where they had just finished work on the Northern Pacific Railroad. Others came from labour contractors in China and Hong Kong. Haney reported that the Chinese workers toiled without complaint when treated fairly, but quit en masse or rioted over the slightest injustice — a penny missing from a paycheque sparked one insurrection.

Haney often travelled 100 miles a day on horseback. On one inspection, he found 2000 Chinese workers sitting idle. After Haney inquired why, the white crew boss told him that one of their comrades had died in a fall into the canyon. The men could see the corpse and would not work nearby. When Haney discovered that the boss had declined to pay an "Indian" ten dollars to get rid of the body, he reprimanded the man for the work stoppage and ordered him to pay the fee. The "Indian's" solution was to steal some dynamite and blasting caps, and to lower the charge by rope into the canyon. The ensuing explosion shredded the corpse. The men returned to work.

Although they did the bulk of the dangerous work in the canyon, Onderdonk paid the Chinese workers less than whites, and provided only meager housing. White labourers received up to $1.75 a day, with room and board supplied. Onderdonk paid the Chinese $1.00 a day, with the stipulation that they purchase food and supplies at his stores. If they bought their supplies elsewhere, they were paid 80 cents a day.

With good reason, the Chinese labourers called the Fraser Canyon "the slaughter pen" — 200 of them died there in 1880. The cemetery at Yale was unable to accommodate the dead. Estimates of the Chinese death toll during construction of the CPR range from 1500 to 3000 — numbers that have given rise to two myths. One of these is outlandish — every railway tie in BC represents one dead Chinese worker; the other is closer to the truth — one Chinese died for every mile of track built in Canada.

A fleet of sternwheelers brought supplies from Port Moody to Onderdonk's railhead at Emory's Bar. Above that point, the Fraser Canyon was considered unnavigable. Because the Cariboo Road was a cliff-hugging thoroughfare, often far above or far below the railway right-of-way, Onderdonk could make only occasional use of it to move materials. The railway track he was constructing became its own supply line, which, coupled with the amount of tunnelling involved, slowed the work.

To reduce dependence on the sternwheelers, Onderdonk, who had taken up residence at Yale, turned the tiny town into a wilderness manufacturing centre. It was a fitting circumstance. In 1868, Yale had been the site of the first public meeting to debate the idea of BC joining Canada. After Onderdonk moved in, Yale soon sported his head office, a nitro factory, a powder plant, a sawmill, and railway shops that turned out rolling stock. When the nitro facility — fortunately situated just outside of town — blew up, it took out every window. Onderdonk promptly had the plant rebuilt.

When the line reached Yale from Emory's Bar on June 7, 1881, the town declared a holiday. Having a rail connection to the dock improved matters, but although nine locomotives plied the track north from Yale, bottlenecks caused delays.

Onderdonk had 600 bridges and many tunnels to construct in advance of the track-laying. Of his two solutions, one was practical, the other mind-boggling. Both typified the manner in which 19th century American industrialists tackled the impossible.

At his Yale sawmill, Onderdonk dedicated a yard to pre-fabricating bridge trestles, built to the specifications of the location engineers. The output of the yard was prolific; some of the trestles installed in the Fraser Canyon late in a day were built from trees that had been growing that morning.

To leapfrog supplies ahead of the track, Onderdonk commissioned the first and only sternwheeler ever to run the heart of the Fraser Canyon. Shipwrights constructed the 127-foot long *Skuzzy* at Spuzzum, 14 miles upriver from Yale. The vessel took to the river with appropriate ceremony on May 4, 1882. On its third attempt — an effort that required almost two weeks — the *Skuzzy* made it through the rapids of Hell's Gate. The vessel inched upstream, assisted by a system of winches and pulleys and by the manpower of 125 Chinese workers who teetered on the cliffs while they yarded lines. The *Skuzzy* subsequently made runs between Boston Bar and Lytton, the ravages of the river dictating repairs during and after each trip. When the railway was completed above Lytton, Onderdonk ordered the *Skuzzy* dismantled and shipped east to Savona's Ferry on Kamloops Lake, where the vessel was reassembled and launched to assist with railway construction.

The terrain above the Fraser Canyon was so steep that

blasting often brought down rockfalls, debris flows, and avalanches. In addition to the often improbable carnage caused by the blasts themselves — one explosion hurled a rock that sank a boat on the Fraser River, drowning one man — these secondary events killed more workers and destroyed equipment and track. One blast-triggered avalanche piled debris 60 feet deep on the line. Crews required five months to clear it. When another blast propagated a rockslide that dammed the North Thompson River, workers took a day off to collect beached salmon and to pan for gold.

Henry Cambie was able to keep the line within the maximum permitted grade of 2.2 percent. But the sinuous courses of the Fraser Canyon forced him to repeatedly exceed the maximum allowable track curvature. Despite the complaints of Marcus Smith, John A. Macdonald's cabinet overlooked the matter to save Onderdonk from even more tunnelling and the government from having to pay extras on the contracts. Onderdonk frequently built wooden trestles over short gaps in the line rather than filling them with rockwork as the contracts specified. This saved time and reduced initial costs, but created a legacy of problems. The construction traffic alone wore out some of the structures. The Liberal critics of the CPR did not miss any of these details. The detractors bellowed when the government awarded Onderdonk's company a fifth contract in 1882 to construct the 85 miles from tidewater at Port Moody to Emory's Bar.

Although he cut corners, Onderdonk was party to at

least one engineering marvel. The 525-foot long Cisco bridge across the Fraser River, south of Lytton, was the second cantilevered bridge installed in North America. The span was built in England, dismantled, and shipped around Cape Horn to Port Moody. When Onderdonk's crews completed the railway line from there to Yale in January 1884, the bridge parts were moved to the installation site. It took five months to reassemble the $269,000 structure, which rested on concrete piers 72 feet high. The CPR removed the bridge in 1909 and shipped it to its E&N Railway on Vancouver Island, where the bridge is still in use.

Despite the spotty quality, the government was pleased that Onderdonk got his work done on time. When Marcus Smith refused to approve the line between Port Moody and Emory's Bar, the government silenced the grousing engineer by transferring him to inspect the half-built track in northern Ontario.

In 1884 the CPR itself awarded Onderdonk's company the final contract in BC, from Savona's Ferry (west of Kamloops) to Eagle Pass in the Monashee Mountains. To any worker who had been employed in the Fraser Canyon, the new contract — with its minimal requirements for tunnels and bridges — must have seemed like a cruise. Onderdonk's men galloped eastward along the grade in 1885, laying track on ties at almost double the specified spacing, until they ran out of steel just shy of Eagle Pass. It had taken them less than nine months to complete 123.1 miles.

Temporary Solutions

Back in the Rockies, where the CPR built its own track, there was trouble in 1883. Van Horne and his construction superintendent, James Ross, were resurveying the line and were reconsidering using Howse Pass to cross the Rockies. When word of their vacillation filtered back to the CPR's head office in Montreal, George Stephen, President of the railway, sought an outside opinion. If history moves in circles, this was a loop that closed quickly. Stephen asked Sandford Fleming if he would again cross the country along the CPR's proposed route to offer a judgment.

Fleming had not been idle since being run off the Pacific Railway project. He had been championing the cause that is his claim to fame: the global implementation of Standard Time. Fleming again invited George Munro Grant to join him. On this journey, the pair saw much that concerned them. They were sobered by the formidable terrain along the north shore of Lake Superior and by the tremendous loss of life in the blasting there.

After a construction work train delivered them to the end-of-steel near Kicking Horse Pass, the men shouldered packs and hoofed it west on the tote road alongside the grade. The road petered out in the lower canyon of the Kicking Horse Valley, where Fleming and Grant were forced to take to a path scarcely a foot wide, 800 feet above the foaming maw of the river. It was a place known as the Golden Stairs — presumably because it was close to the boomtown of Golden City. Fleming later wrote: "I do not think that I can ever forget that terrible walk; it was the greatest trial I ever experienced." Grant echoed the sentiment: "It seemed as if a false step would have hurled us to the base, to certain death." Surveyor Charles Shaw had been descending the Golden Stairs earlier in the year, when he met two men heading up the path with a packhorse. There was insufficient room for the groups to pass each other or to turn the horse around. So after cutting the packboxes away, the men pushed the horse off the cliff.

After recuperating for a few days at First Crossing on the Columbia River (now Donald), Fleming's party traversed Rogers Pass. They required only a day to reach the height of land. Following the slash line of the survey, the men covered 24 miles next day. Only 17 miles remained to Second Crossing on the Columbia River (now Revelstoke), but it took them five days. Grant lamented the "unutterable loneliness of savage mountains" through which "there was nothing even to guide, save an occasional glimpse of the sun, and the slate-coloured, churned up torrent...."

Fleming concluded that neither Kicking Horse Pass nor Rogers Pass was a promising place in which to build a railway. Nonetheless, on the basis of a trial survey run by Charles Shaw late in 1883 (see Prologue), James Ross rejected the longer alternative of going over Howse Pass and around the hairpin bend of the Columbia River. In November 1883, with no other viable option to consider and with the end-of-steel already poised at the crest of Kicking Horse Pass, George Stephen was forced to accept Major Rogers' line as the best route through the Rockies and the Selkirks.

Van Horne and Ross knew that the construction effort of 1884 would make or break the CPR. From Kicking Horse Pass to the Columbia River, the line ran for only 49.4 miles. But it was a piece of country jammed with construction evils: sidehills, avalanche slopes, canyons, tunnels, and nine crossings of the Kicking Horse River. To keep to the permitted grade by following Major Rogers' route, the CPR would have required at least two years and would have spent upwards of $4 million. Taking a suggestion from Sandford Fleming, Van Horne proposed a "temporary solution." He petitioned the government to allow the CPR to run the rails straight down the hill west from Kicking Horse Pass at more than double the permitted grade. Van Horne promised that the CPR would reduce the grade after the railway opened for business.

The government reluctantly complied, authorizing a 4.5 percent grade on four miles of track west of Kicking Horse Pass, and grades approaching four percent just west of present day Field. The 4.5 percent grade — which amounted to free-fall for locomotives and rolling stock equipped with manual brakes — became the steepest, sustained, standard-gauge incline of its era, anywhere in the world.

In the spring of 1884, "help wanted" signs appeared on main streets across western Canada and the U.S. Midwest.

The CPR required 12,000 men to shovel, pry, hack, and blast the grade from the mountainsides of the Kicking Horse Valley. Morley Roberts was among those who responded. With a bundle of blankets, but no money to his name, Roberts took passage on a CPR work train from Winnipeg. An agent rousted Roberts and a hundred others from the train just east of Kicking Horse Pass and instructed them to follow the tote road until they found a contractor who required them.

Roberts and a companion headed west, fording rivers and scrambling across the stringers of half-built bridges. Roberts went to work for the Corey Brothers, whose gang was constructing a 300-foot mud tunnel in the lower canyon. His work arrangement was typical. In the mountains, the contractors paid $2.25 for a 10-hour day (as opposed to the $1.50 a day paid on the prairies), but took back $5.00 per week for board. Workers could purchase supplies from the contractor's store, but at greatly inflated prices. The workers slept in any manner of tents, lean-tos, cabins, or on the ground, with whatever clothing and blankets they had brought.

Building a railway in the mountains with pick and shovel was hungry work, as a provisions manifest from 1884 attested. The monthly staples provided to a crew of five included: 125 lbs. of bacon, 65 lbs. of ham, one-half a barrel of corned beef, 26 lbs. of sugar, 10 lbs. of tea, 5 lbs. of coffee, 30 lbs. of oatmeal, 25 lbs. of beans, 12 lbs. of split peas, 20 lbs. of rice, and two dozen other items. The men occasionally received fresh meat, usually horses or oxen killed in accidents.

Construction in the Kicking Horse Canyon was brutal, dangerous toil that, according to a local newspaper, claimed lives at the rate of "about one per week." In 1884, the labourers moved 1,500,000 cubic yards of rock and soil, drilled half a mile of tunnels, and built 11 major bridges, completing 67 miles of line. The Ottertail River bridge was a marvel — 700 feet long and incorporating 295,000 board feet of lumber. Instead of carving the railbed into the mountainsides, contractors saved money by constructing rickety cribworks called "grasshopper trestles."

Van Horne's "temporary solution" to the steep grade of Kicking Horse Pass soon became known as the Big Hill. The incline was christened with blood when the first construction train to back down the grade ran away, launched from a curve, and crashed into the river, killing three workers. To counter the threat to men and machines, the CPR installed three safety switches and spur tracks at roughly 1-mile intervals on the hill. Staffed at all hours, the switches were set to divert westbound trains onto the spurs, which were angled upslope away from the main line to assist with braking.

When a work train passed a marker board 1000 feet from a safety switch, the locomotive engineer gave one long whistle blast to alert the switchman. When 300 feet from the switch, the engineer gave four short blasts to indicate that the train was under control. If the switchman did not hear the four blasts or if he thought that the train was going too fast, he did not throw the switch. The train would run onto the spur where, as one worker commented, "wrecks could take place without hindering traffic on the main line."

The system sometimes failed. When another construction train ran away, a sleepy switchman thought that he had heard the four short whistle blasts. He threw the #3 switch. Despite frantic braking efforts by the crew, the train overran the switch. Ahead was the "nose tunnel," where 60 men were working, and then a 2-mile run on the main line to the yard at Field. The crew leapt from the train. Disaster was averted when the tender (firewood car) derailed, dragging the runaway to a destructive halt before the tunnel.

The Big Hill was anything but temporary. It endured for more than 23 years, until the CPR completed the two Spiral Tunnels, which doubled the length of the line on the hill and reduced the maximum grade to 2.43 percent. The tunnels took two years to construct and cost $1.5 million. Although railway workers died operating trains on the Big Hill, not a single passenger was killed. This was pure luck. In the early 1900s, passenger trains — running elsewhere on much gentler grades — killed an average of 70 people a year in Canada.

The Big Hill did provide the CPR with one lucrative benefit. Because it proved costly and dangerous to haul heavy dining cars up and down the grade, Van Horne decreed that a restaurant car would be parked at Field. When the first tourists stepped off the train for meals in 1886, they were enthralled with the scenery. Van Horne hit upon the idea of building Mt. Stephen House — the first of seven hotels that the CPR constructed in the mountains of Alberta and BC.

Match Sticks and Nightshifts

In the tight terrain of the Selkirk Mountains, the sideslopes traversed by the CPR were often much steeper than those in the Rockies. In a distance of 6.2 miles on the eastern approach to Rogers Pass, six streams bisected the grade in their plunges to the Beaver River. The CPR bridged three of these — Mountain Creek, Surprise Creek, and Stoney Creek — with spectacular spans that soon became the most celebrated on the line.

The bridge across Mountain Creek was among the larger wooden structures ever built. Its deck was 154 feet above the creek, 1086 feet long, and incorporated more than two million board feet of lumber. The Surprise Creek bridge was 406 feet long and 180 feet high. But in this landscape of dizzying drops, the deck of the Stoney Creek bridge took the crown — at its central pier, it towered more than 228 feet above the creek.

As James Ross described in a letter to Van Horne in 1885, the footings for two of the bridges posed great problems: "Surprise and Stoney foundations are heartbreaking! The rock is so uncertain and unsatisfactory that it has been a very difficult matter to make good foundations there." The structures required so much time — the Stoney Creek bridge took seven weeks to complete — that Ross used electric lights to run a nightshift, the first recorded instance in railway construction in North America.

The wooden bridges — built on grades of roughly two percent — terrified construction workers and locomotive engineers. Three stories concerning these structures and the CPR's General Manager have endured. When he traversed Rogers Pass on foot in 1884, Van Horne's party came to the partially completed Mountain Creek bridge. A few days earlier, several workers had fallen from its deck to their deaths, prompting Van Horne's companions to crawl across the span on loose planks above the abyss. Van Horne, however, strode over and back, and over again. The following year, when Van Horne visited the site of the Stoney Creek bridge, he got a firsthand taste of the difficulties that James Ross had described. Workers were desperately attempting to shore up the footings from the effects of the surging creek. In a classic example of a hands-on managerial style, Van Horne joined the men, waist-deep in the creek and the muck, moving timbers and boulders to help save the bridge. Van Horne later rode in the cab of a work train in Rogers Pass. When the engineer voiced his concern about the safety of an upcoming bridge, Van Horne responded: "Here, get down and I'll take her over myself."

Fire threatened wooden structures everywhere on the CPR — in some cases before construction began. Fourteen boxcars loaded with timber for the Stoney Creek bridge burned in a forest fire while parked on a siding near the bridge site, dealing a two-week setback to construction. James Ross wrote to Van Horne: "I consider it would be a good idea to put a tank at a large bridge like Mountain Creek and have two lines of pipe run over it, with [stop]cocks to be used during the dry season...." Yet no system more elaborate than a few barrels of water was in place when the Stoney Creek bridge caught fire in July 1886. A handful of workers saved the bridge, but the fire consumed the Atlantic Express, the second eastbound passenger train to cross Rogers Pass.

Van Horne had doubts as to the strength of the wooden spans. Not long after the trio of bridges was completed, he ordered their trestle works filled. With the steep creeks nearby, the lofty bridges were ideal for the application of a new technology — hydraulic filling. By diverting creek water into spillways, into which workers dumped rock and soil, engineers were able to direct sluices of watery fill into the trestle cribworks. When the water trickled out, the fill set-up like concrete. It was a brilliant solution, but not enough to meet the demands of increasing traffic and heavier locomotives. The CPR replaced all three bridges with steel structures and extensive approach filling — Stoney Creek in 1893, Surprise Creek in 1896, and Mountain Creek in 1902.

When the rails crested Rogers Pass on August 17, 1885, it was as much a cause for concern as for celebration. It had taken almost six months to construct 31.9 miles. West of the pass, Major Rogers' line dropped at a grade of nearly 4.5 percent for the first 3.5 miles. Unlike at Kicking Horse Pass, Van

Horne had not requested permission from the government to construct the line with such a steep grade. The only solution was to lengthen the track. James Ross gave the problem to an assistant engineer, Sammy Sykes. His solution was another engineering marvel — The Loops.

Sykes added almost four miles to the line in the upper valley of the Illecillewaet River by looping the rails into two sidevalleys. The grade revision incorporated four mammoth wooden trestles, six river crossings, and 14 snowsheds, but also routed the line away from some of the worst avalanche paths. Ross realized that Van Horne would find the scale of the new construction alarming: "I regret being obliged to submit this line [for your approval] but there are so many objectionable features on the present location [Major Rogers' line] and the more you examine them, the less you like them...." Ross's final selling points were surprising: The Loops would have less curvature and would be $500,000 cheaper to build than the other proposed grade. The CPR strengthened the trestles of The Loops with fill in 1900, and replaced the wooden structures with steel spans on stone piers in 1913. Although abandoned when the Connaught Tunnel opened in 1916, the piers survive, a testimony to the Italian masons who constructed them.

The location engineers knew that the line in Rogers Pass repeatedly crossed avalanche slopes, but there was no time at the end of the 1885 season to build snowsheds. Van Horne stationed three engineers in camps near the pass that winter to record where avalanches threatened the track. He planned to construct snowsheds over those sections in the spring of 1886, before the railway opened for business.

It was a naïve approach to the most formidable threat anywhere on the railway. More than 50 feet of snow fell each year in the Selkirks. Many of the avalanche paths were several miles long and dropped thousands of feet. The slide debris could choke the valley bottoms, with accompanying wind blasts violent enough to snap trees and knock loaded freight cars from the rails. Before the line was built, workers had received an inkling of the peril. On February 8, 1885, three massive slides swept the grade just west of Rogers Pass, killing one man and burying three others, destroying two camps and a building.

When the observers made their reports in 1886, Van Horne must have pounded his desk with frustration. In one winter, avalanches had destroyed six miles of the newly completed track. One section had been buried nine times. At another location, the track was covered by avalanche debris 39 feet deep. The debris of another slide contained 120,000 cubic yards of snow. To protect his railway, Van Horne spent more than $1 million in 1886 constructing 54 snowsheds that consumed almost 19 million board feet of lumber to cover more than five miles of track. This remedy, which delayed the commercial opening of the CPR, was not entirely successful. Some of the sheds were not long enough. The following winter, avalanched snow spilled around their ends, plugging the track. Snow and boulders crushed other sheds. Some sections of track not swept by avalanches in the winter of 1885-86 were buried in subsequent winters.

The snowsheds were a solution that brought its own set of problems. The sheds were firetraps, threatened by sparks from locomotives and by forest fires. To reduce the risk and to improve the views for tourists, Van Horne laid open track for summer use. Some of the sheds were on the valley floor, away from the mountainsides. Van Horne buried these valley sheds to strengthen them, effectively creating tunnels. Smoke from locomotives would linger in the sheds, so design engineers tried to strike the balance between minimum length and maximum efficiency, but not always successfully. Lastly, steam would condense on the shed ceilings in winter, then drip to the rails and freeze, causing a loss of traction for the locomotives whose efficiency was already hampered by the steep grades.

In 1888, the CPR took possession of six rotary plows to deal with the avalanche debris in Rogers Pass. With labourers shoveling ahead of them, these early snowblowers could cut 40-foot deep swaths. But some deposits were so deep, consolidated, and interlaced with so many broken trees, that only blasting would remove them.

The various incarnations of the Rogers Pass station illustrated the avalanche threat. The original siding was at the crest of Rogers Pass. Within a year, the CPR built a new siding two miles to the north. In January 1899, an avalanche destroyed the station, killing eight of the ten people inside, including the stationmaster, his wife, and his two children. The woman was found with a rolling pin in one hand and pastry in the other. It could have been worse; many other resident employees were away clearing another slide. Two railway superintendents would have been aboard a train in the yard at the time, but locomotive trouble had delayed their arrival.

The CPR moved the station again, this time one mile closer to the pass. After a decade with no avalanches at that location, the CPR laid open track to bypass the #17 snowshed. In March 1910, a slide came down from the west, launched off the abandoned snowshed, and buried 600 feet of the new line. The CPR held eastbound and westbound passenger trains at nearby sidings and dispatched a gang of Japanese labourers to the site to assist a rotary plow in excavating the debris.

While they were working in the early evening, another slide came down, this one from Avalanche Mountain to the east. It covered the same 600 feet of track to a depth of 30 feet, entombing all of the Japanese workers and killing one of the train crew. Only four people escaped. The slide was so powerful, it ripped the locomotive and the rotary plow apart and flung the 100-ton plow onto the roof of the snowshed — 40 feet above and 60 feet away from the line. More than 500 feet of the snowshed was "splintered like match wood." Many of the dead were found still standing. One group of three faced each other, caught in mid-conversation. One of the men held a pipe in his hand.

This tragedy — 62 dead — remains the greatest loss of life in a single avalanche in Canada. But it was not the reason that the CPR planned the 5-mile long Connaught Tunnel beneath Rogers Pass. The tunnel had already been on the drawing board to reduce the grade.

Done Well in Every Way

At the beginning of 1885, a 220-mile gap separated James Ross's westbound work gangs at Beavermouth from Andrew Onderdonk's eastbound work gangs at Savona's Ferry. Because Onderdonk's route followed easier terrain, Van Horne assumed that he would build 120 miles, while Ross would build 100 miles. Onderdonk's crews were provisioned from the west accordingly and quit work on September 28 when they ran out of steel. The pressure was now on James Ross to complete the crossings of Rogers Pass and Eagle Pass, so that the cash-strapped CPR could be opened for business. His crews reached the east bank of the Columbia River at Second Crossing (now Revelstoke) on October 8. Ross knew that his men would soon encounter snow. He rallied them to build the remaining 27.8 miles with tremendous speed, again employing electric lights to run a night shift.

The completion of the CPR brought together a cast of barons and builders, engineers and everyman, in what was — given the innumerable delays of the preceding year — a miracle of timing. Late in August, Van Horne anticipated that Ross would complete the line in early- or mid-autumn. But when pressed for details about the attendant ceremony and who would be invited, Van Horne replied characteristically: "The last spike will be just as good an iron one as there is between Montreal and Vancouver, and anyone who wants to see it driven will have to pay full fare."

In September, Van Horne learned that Lord Lansdowne, the Governor General, was planning a trip across Canada that would take him to Vancouver in early October. His Excellency wondered if he might be in the right place at the right time to drive the last spike, and even went so far as to have a silver spike minted. Van Horne placed the Governor General's itinerary before James Ross as an incentive to get the work done quickly. After Lansdowne had gone west over the gap in the line, Ross wired Van Horne:

OWING TO UNSETTLED STATES OF THE WEATHER I CANNOT GUARANTEE TO FINISH TRACK IN TIME SO IT WOULD BE WELL TO COMMUNICATE WITH HIS EXCELLENCY AT VICTORIA.

The Governor General would miss the completion of the CPR, as would the government's Chief Engineer, Collingwood Schreiber, and its Minister of Railways and Canals, Charles Tupper. The pair of bureaucrats had launched a Pacific junket hoping to gatecrash the ceremony, but they were too early.

When newspaper reporters discovered that an official train would be heading west in the autumn, they again pressed Van Horne for details of a ceremony. The general finally lost his cool while replying to a reporter in Winnipeg: "Our trip has nothing to do with the opening of the [rail]road. It is … just the usual trip of inspection before the winter sets in… We intend going to British Columbia, but cannot say whether we will pass over the line before or after the last spike, about which you appear to be so anxious, is driven. No, I'm sure I can't say who will drive the last spike. It may be Tom Mularky or Joe Tubby, and the only ceremony I fancy may occur will be the damning of the foreman for not driving it quicker. There will be no concluding ceremony, no nonsense." No nonsense certainly, but there would be an impromptu ceremony.

On November 6, Ross's track-laying crew, under the direction of Frank Brothers, tackled the remaining 3.5-mile gap on the line. By 3:20 p.m., the workers had laid just over three miles of track when they ran out of rails. The supply train returned to Second Crossing. At 9:00 p.m., the train again rattled west over the hastily built track to the last end-of-steel on the CPR mainline. On the way, the crew had to abandon a flat car of rails because the train could not make it up one section of snow-covered grade. Work recommenced under electric lights and continued until Brothers was certain that what remained could be completed early next morning. Brothers had burned the candle because the official train, carrying Van Horne, other members of the CPR executive, and a few dignitaries, had arrived at Second Crossing earlier that day.

Saturday, November 7, 1885 dawned grey. Mist shrouded

Eagle Pass, and snow cloaked the trees. It was not a poster day for a ceremony, but it was fitting because so much of the CPR had been built in conditions far from ideal. Long before that day, Van Horne had determined that the railway's point of completion would be named Craigellachie (creg-AH-lack-ee), after a rock in Scotland's Spey Valley. Craigellachie, which means "rock of alarm," was the traditional gathering place of the Clan Grant. CPR President George Stephen and his cousin, Donald Smith, also on the CPR executive, were descendants of that Clan. The pair had often used the Clan's cry, "Stand fast Craigellachie!" in correspondence during the many tribulations of financing the railway.

Van Horne's official train arrived at the end-of-steel just before 9:00 a.m., as Major Rogers — eager as ever to be in on the action — cut the two sections of rail that would complete the line. Those on hand had taken bets as to what length the final rails would be. They measured 25 feet, 5 inches — all that remained of 2893 miles. Navvies spiked the rails at their eastern ends. As the dignitaries gathered and photographer Alex Ross set up, Major Rogers drove spikes to secure the west end of the southerly rail.

George Stephen, CPR President, was in London attempting to acquire a Royal Mail contract for the railway. In his place, Van Horne asked Donald Smith to drive the last spike. Smith, who had spent almost a third of his life at a Labrador fur trade outpost, now controlled the Hudson's Bay Company and the Bank of Montreal, and was the most powerful businessman in Canada. John A. Macdonald would have seen the irony of Smith's act, and no doubt Van Horne intended him to. Smith was a former Conservative member of parliament who, in 1873, had voted against Macdonald in the confidence motion over the Pacific Scandal. Now Smith would wield the maul that made real the Prime Minister's long held dream.

The navvies present at Craigellachie may well have chuckled at Smith's efforts. Although the last spike had been half-driven for him, Smith bent it with the first blow. Frank Brothers extracted the now second-to-last spike, setting another in place. It was 9:22 a.m. Smith tapped carefully until certain that the metal would take, and then swung the maul confidently.

With the job done, the crowd turned expectantly to Van Horne, who had been standing at Smith's elbow. Although some in the throng had hitched a ride to the site on the last construction train, there was not a single hanger-on or politician among them. All had earned a place, either by toil, by nerve, or by stamina untold. This was a ceremony as utilitarian as could have been planned. In addition to Major Rogers, Tom Wilson was there, as was Henry Cambie, James Ross, John Egan, Sam Steele, and — more than 23 years after he had advanced the idea of a transcontinental railway — Sandford Fleming. Van Horne had accomplished the impossible five and a half years ahead of schedule and could have played up to the moment. But he dispatched it with customary efficiency: "All that I can say is that the work has been done well in every way."

The Honourable Donald A. Smith drives the last spike
to complete the Canadian Pacific Railway. Van Horne
is to the left of Smith; Sandford Fleming is behind.

As the dignitaries made their way to the train, the locomotive's whistle wailed, and a brief pandemonium erupted
among the common folk at railside. Major Rogers attempted
to mark the place by picking up an unused railroad tie to drive
into the half-frozen ground. One of the navvies approached
the site of Donald Smith's work, spike and maul in hand, and
sarcastically announced: "Now for the real last spike." He
drove one home. Others took the maul and, by turns, filled
the wood with spikes until it could hold no more.

Just before the conductor proclaimed, "All aboard for
the Pacific!", a worker handed the maul to Donald Smith as

a memento. Smith also demanded the bent spike, which Van Horne's secretary had picked up. Parts of the spike were later incorporated into pieces of family jewelry.

Following the ceremony, the official train set off at a clip, travelling at an average of 57 miles per hour to North Bend in the Fraser Canyon. Sam Steele was aboard the last car. He reported that it "whipped around the sharp curves like the tail of a kite." As a result, all but three of the car's passengers were motion-sick.

Cameras were not commonplace in 1885, especially not to construction workers in the wilds of BC. In other images from that era, work stopped and eyes stared into the lens whenever a camera appeared at railside. It testifies to the importance of the last spike ceremony that, of the 50 or so people framed in Canada's most famous photograph, few looked into the camera as the shutter opened to record the moment when Donald Smith completed the CPR mainline. The remainder leaned forward, peered over shoulders, and balanced on tiptoes, necks craning for a glimpse of a history concluded and a history beginning.

Chapter 10
The Road of a Thousand Wonders

U nlike the CPR and the Canadian Northern, which cut corners in construction, Charles Melville Hays built the Grand Trunk Pacific on the principle that "the first cost will be the last." He did not want to have service soon interrupted for mandatory improvements, as had been the case with the CPR.

It was a sound theory, but it collapsed because the GTPR built through largely unsettled and rugged land, at a cost that far exceeded estimates and with the tracks of the rival Canadian Northern paralleling it for much of the way. Even with the proceeds from partial service between Winnipeg and Edmonton, the GTPR lacked the business it needed to pay off its staggering construction costs.

The Road of a Thousand Wonders

In the election year of 1911, Wilfred Laurier's government loaned the struggling railway $10 million in an attempt to paint a brighter picture for voters. Hays wanted to direct the money to grandiose schemes, but the cash soon disappeared into paying bills. He began to pull back from plans for a Pacific steamship service and for branch lines — including one that would have linked Hazelton and Alaska. He also eliminated a proposal for a chain of hotels. His pitch that the GTPR was to be "The Road of a Thousand Wonders" began to sound hollow.

Laurier's government fell in December 1911, ending 15 years of Liberal rule. Robert Borden led the incoming Conservatives. The new Prime Minister had been a Canadian Northern supporter all along and, in a curious departure from typical party preferences, advocated public control of national railways. It was clear to Hays that the GTPR would not receive more government loans.

In February 1912, Hays and his family sailed for London. In protracted sessions with the Grand Trunk executive, Hays attempted to save his railway from bankruptcy. Records of the meetings have not survived, but it is likely that the executive instructed Hays to divorce the GTPR from the National Transcontinental, leaving the Canadian government to deal with the unviable section of line through northern Ontario and central Quebec. We shall never know whether Hays intended to follow such direction, for he and his family sailed for New York aboard the *Titanic*. After ushering his wife and daughter to a lifeboat, Hays was among the 1513 souls who perished in the space of 14 minutes, early on the morning of April 15, 1912.

Two contrary myths have endured concerning the death of Charles Melville Hays. One purports that he went to the bottom of the Atlantic bearing papers that contained the secret for saving the GTPR. The other holds that his body was retrieved with such papers in a coat pocket. The body of Hays was indeed among the 328 recovered, but no such papers were found. He was buried at Montreal.

The government completed the National Transcontinental on November 17, 1913. On April 6, 1914, the GTPR's construction crews came within a mile of each other, just east of Fort Fraser in central BC. Next day, the two gangs staged a race to see which would be the first to lay a half-mile of track. The westbound crew won by a few minutes. Its foreman, Peter Titiryn, drove the last spike. After eight years and eight months — six years of which had been required to build the 416 miles from Prince Rupert — the GTPR had the run of steel from coast to coast.

It all went sour immediately. Hays's replacement, Edson Chamberlin, informed the government that, because the National Transcontinental had been completed at a cost of $160 million — $100 million over estimates — the GTPR would not honour its obligation to pay rent, which was calculated as a percentage of construction costs. It was a legitimate and convenient out, but the truth was that the GTPR could not afford to pay any rent.

Business for the GTPR had collapsed. Grain, lumber, and minerals — the staple freights of a northern railway — were in low demand abroad. Immigration had all but stopped. The Panama Canal had opened, turning Vancouver into a bustling port at the expense of any new commerce that might have gone the way of Prince Rupert. The GTPR's development company had sold fewer lots than it retained. The beginning of WWI in September 1914 destroyed any hope for an immediate economic turnaround and precluded further financing from Britain. Prime Minister Borden refused another loan. In 1915, the President of the GTPR washed his hands of the venture when he asked the Canadian government to take over the railway.

On January 23, 1915, the Canadian Northern drove its last spike at Basque, near Kamloops in southern BC. In the span of 15 years, while Canada's population had increased 40 percent, its railway mileage had increased 130 percent. The country now had 30,000 miles of track, ranking it fifth in the world and first as an expression of miles per capita.

The Canadian Northern was, for much the same reasons as the GTPR, in desperate straits. Borden's government was more concerned with the homegrown venture. If the Canadian Northern had collapsed and taken down the Canadian Bank of Commerce — its principal backer — the repercussions for the country would have been disastrous. As if forgetting how much public money and land it had received during its construction, the CPR griped that, if the government bailed out the GTPR and the Canadian Northern, the CPR would be a private venture forced to compete with companies on the public dole.

Borden's solution to what everyone was calling "the railway problem" was to appoint that defining Canadian institution — a Royal Commission. Its findings, released in 1916, recommended that the government nationalize and consolidate the Grand Trunk, GTPR, and Canadian Northern. And so Canadian National Railways came into being. The process was not completed until 1923, by which time the new railway included 22,110 miles of track and employed more than 99,000 workers, making Canadian National the single largest industrial employer in Canada. It began operations with a $1.3 billion debt.

During the amalgamation, Borden's government favoured the interests of the Canadian Northern, appointing David Hanna, a former Canadian Northern Vice-President, as Canadian National's first boss. Where the tracks of the GTPR and Canadian Northern ran close together, Hanna ordered the tracks of the better-built GTPR torn up. The rails were supposed to be sent to France for use in the war in 1917, but there is no record that the steel was shipped. In what can only be viewed as an act of spite, Canadian National subsequently lifted the Canadian Northern's rails and placed them on the GTPR's empty rail bed.

Where the tracks of the GTPR and Canadian Northern diverged at Red Pass Junction in BC, Canadian National took over both spurs — one to Vancouver to compete success-fully with the CPR, the other to Prince Rupert in the hope of a boom that so far has not materialized. In a final irony, 50 years later, much of the GTPR's abandoned grade through the Rockies finally became a road of wonders — in many places, the Yellowhead Highway follows the old railbed.

Epilogue

When Robert M. Rylatt signed on as storekeeper with Walter Moberly' survey party in July 1871, his contract indentured him for two years. But after learning of his wife's death in October 1872, Rylatt began pestering his boss to release him. Moberly complied in May the following year. To Rylatt and a companion, Harry Baird, Moberly gave three horses and an advance against the expenses of the trip back to civilization. The pair set off from near the site of present-day Jasper, to cross Yellowhead Pass and to make their way along the North Thompson River to Fort Kamloops.

The journey was a month of pure adventure. Rylatt was wracked by scurvy, his mouth sore, his gums bleeding. He resorted to eating the roots of swamp vegetation. The men were frequently in and out of makeshift canoes and rafts, sometimes barely surviving the river crossings. After one such epic on the North Thompson River, Rylatt permitted himself — for the first time — to speculate on the cause of his labours and hardships with the Pacific Survey.

"While drying our clothing, and letting the animals browse (by the way, Harry has burned his moccasins by putting them too near the fire), we fell to cogitating on the possibilities and probabilities of the Canadian Pacific Railroad. And in the minds [sic] eye we pictured a train of cars sweeping along over this flat; over the fierce streams we had passed; puffing and snorting up the mountain sides in gentle curves and windings, shrieking wildly as some denison [denizen] of the forest, scared at the strange monster of fire and smoke, and only anxious to put distance between itself and this strange monster, is hurrying off at a greater speed as the shrill whistle reaches it, at the wearied looks in the eyes of the passengers, longing for the end of the route, yet rallying for a few brief minutes at the sound of the whistle, and [the] sight of the frightened animal...."

From Fort Kamloops, Rylatt carried on to Yale, BC, bumping along a wagon road in what must have seemed the epitome of comfortable travel — a stagecoach. He completed his journey home to New Westminster by steamer on the Fraser River.

It would be interesting to know if Robert M. Rylatt ever travelled by railway on the route through the mountains that he had helped to survey, and, if so, what he thought of that journey. But history has left us no such account.

Author's Notes

Although Canada adopted metric measurement in 1971, its railways continue to have mile boards and to weigh their locomotives in tons and their rails in pounds per yard. As a book about railways necessarily includes a great many numbers — dates, distances, speeds, quantities, and weights — I have elected to use Imperial measurement to ensure integrity and accuracy, and to minimize cluttering with conversions.

Imperial	Metric
1 lb.	0.454 kg
1 inch	2.54 cm
1 foot	0.3048 m
1 yard	0.9144 m
1 mile	1.6093 km
1 ton	1.016 t
1 square mile	2.59 km^2

Canada's first transcontinental railway, the Canadian Pacific, did not receive that name until 1882. I refer to the surveying and construction efforts of 1871-1881 as those of the Pacific Railway, which — although no such railway was chartered — is what the people of the day called it.

I refer to railway workers and officials as "men" because I found no references to women being employed in the construction forces or in the hierarchies of the Canadian Pacific, Grand Trunk Pacific, and Canadian Northern railways.

Further Reading

Bain, Donald M. *Canadian Pacific in the Rockies.* Calgary: British Railway Modellers of North America, (ten volume bind-up) 1985.

Berton, Pierre. *The National Dream.* Toronto: McClelland and Stewart, 1970.

Berton, Pierre. *The Last Spike.* McClelland and Stewart, 1971.

Bickersteth, J. Burgon. *The Land of Open Doors.* Toronto: University of Toronto Press, reprint 1976.

Blaise, Clark. *Time Lord: Sir Sandford Fleming and the Creation of Standard Time.* New York: Pantheon Books, 2000.

Bone, P. Turner. *When the Steel Went Through.* Toronto: The MacMillan Company of Canada Ltd., 1947.

Booth, Jan. *Canadian Pacific in the Selkirks: 100 Years in Rogers Pass.* Calgary: British Railway Modellers of North America, 2nd edition, 1991.

Buck, George H. *From Summit to Sea.* Calgary: Fifth House, 1997.

Cruise, David and Alison Griffiths. *Lords of the Line.* Markham: Penguin Books, 1989.

Grant, Rev. George M. *Ocean to Ocean.* Edmonton: M.G. Hurtig Ltd., reprint 1967.

Green, Lorne. *Chief Engineer.* Toronto: Dundurn Press, 1993.

Lavallée, Omer. *Van Horne's Road.* Montreal: Railfare Books, 1974.

Leonard, Frank. *A Thousand Blunders: The Grand Trunk Pacific Railway and Northern British Columbia.* Vancouver: UBC Press, 1996.

MacKay, Donald. *The Asian Dream.* Vancouver/Toronto: Douglas and McIntyre, 1986.

McKee, Bill and Georgeen Klassen. *Trail of Iron.* Calgary: Glenbow-Alberta Institute, 1983.

Moberly, Walter. *Early History of the C.P.R. Road* [1909]. Manuscript HE 2810 C2M55, Robarts Library, University of Toronto.

Pole, Graeme. *The Spiral Tunnels and the Big Hill.* Canmore: Altitude Publishing, 1996.

Roberts, Morley. *The Western Avernus.* London: J.M. Dent & Sons Ltd, n.d.

Further Reading

Rylatt, R.M. *Surveying the Canadian Pacific.* Salt Lake City: University of Utah Press, 1991.

Secretan, J.H.E. *Canada's Great Highway: From the First Stake to the Last Spike.* London: John Lane the Bodley Head Ltd., 1924.

Shaw, Charles Æneas. *Tales of a Pioneer Surveyor.* Don Mills: Longman Canada Ltd., 1970.

Sleigh, Daphne. *Walter Moberly and the Northwest Passage by Rail.* Surrey: Hancock House Publishers Ltd., 2003.

Talbot, F.A. *The Making of a Great Canadian Railway.* Toronto: The Musson Book Company Limited, 1912.

Turner, Robert. D. *West of the Great Divide.* Winlaw: Sono Nis, 2nd edition, 2003.

Wilson, Ralph and Don Thomas. *The Line.* Calgary: Canadian Pacific Railway, 1998.

Wilson, Thomas E. *Trail Blazer of the Canadian Rockies.* Calgary: Glenbow-Alberta Institute, 1982.

Yeats, Floyd. *Canadian Pacific's Big Hill.* Calgary: British Railway Modellers of North America, 1985.

Acknowledgments

I thank Rick Collier, Marnie Pole, and Mardy Roberts for commenting on the first draft, and for collectively preventing several significant derailments.

About the Author

Graeme Pole has been writing about the human history and the natural history of western Canada since 1989. This is his ninth book. He lives with his family near Hazelton in northwestern BC, where he serves as a paramedic. Visit his website: www.mountainvision.ca

Photo Credits